VOICES OF
THE SELF

African American Life Series

VOICES OF THE SELF

A Study of

Language

Competence

KEITH GILYARD

 Wayne State University Press   Detroit

Library of Congress Cataloging-in-Publication Data

Gilyard, Keith, 1952–
    Voices of the self : a study of language competence / Keith
Gilyard.
        p.   cm. — (African American life)
    Includes bibliographical references and index.
    ISBN 0-8143-2224-7 (alk. paper). — ISBN 0-8143-2225-5
(pbk. : alk. paper)
        1. Sociolinguistics — United States. 2. Gilyard, Keith, 1952–   —
Childhood and youth. 3. Afro-Americans — Languages. 4. Afro-
Americans — Education. 5. English language — Social aspects — United
States. I. Title. II. Series.
P40.45.U5G55 1991
306.4′4 — dc20   90-24737

    The essay portions of this book were written under
the auspices of the Program in English Education at
New York University.
    Special thanks to Gordon Pradl.

Designer: Joanne Elkin Kinney

To
Andre, Taneha, Kahlil, Kaamilah,
Matthew, Tyrell, Jerome,
Amina, Asha,
and Tiffany

Contents

1
Introduction

Over the past quarter century few problems in education have received as much media, professional, and parental attention as the fact that, by and large, young urban African-Americans have not achieved Standard English competence in public schools. The reasons for this are complex and, as expected, explanations abound and many solutions have been readily proposed. But there have been few, if any, unqualified success stories, and the proponents of theory themselves have been vehemently at odds with one another.

Such writers as Geneva Smitherman (1977), Jim Haskins and Hugh Butts (1973), and J. L. Dillard (1973) have condemned the public school system's traditional nonrecognition and nonacceptance of the separate and legitimate language variety, popularly labeled Black English, spoken by the majority of inner-city Black youth.* In their view, this implicit and explicit rejection of language communicates a rejection of both Black children and the culture that has produced them. The school characteristically fails, the argument continues, to capitalize on the linguistic competencies the children have already developed. When, predictably, these students seem less than enthusiastic about formal education, they are portrayed as slow learners. Little is expected of them academically, and academically these students produce very little — yet another example of the self-fulfilling prophecy.

*Although "African-American" and "Black" are used interchangeably, the author acknowledges that the former term is more accurate.

The use of Black English in schools, therefore, has seemed plausible to many educators. One response, for example, was the 1974 resolution passed by members of the Conference on College Composition and Communication advocating the "students' right to their own language." Of course such resolutions, not being binding, are frequently ignored. Legions of teachers and other citizens (many of them Black) have considered all this talk about Black English to be mere "Black nonsense" and have insisted all along that there is no place for Black English, if such a thing exists, in the curriculum. Marva Collins, for one, founded a private school in Chicago in which any positive mention of Black English is eschewed. Her approach has been heralded by many, and her story was the subject of a docudrama that appeared on national television. In a similar vein, conservatives inside the National Council of Teachers of English have conspired to abrogate the students' right resolution (see Sledd 1983).

However, keeping in spirit with Smitherman, Haskins, Butts, Dillard, and company, Judge Charles W. Joiner ruled, in a precedent-setting case in 1979, that Black English is indeed a distinct linguistic form and must have an officially established place within the educational environment of the Martin Luther King Jr. Elementary School in Ann Arbor, Michigan. Joiner's decision was hailed as a great victory by those who considered themselves progressive.

Throughout all these developments, amid this cacophony of voices, African-American students in large numbers continue not to master Standard English. Oddly enough, conspicuously absent are the voices of the students themselves. I am not speaking about the street stories or the recorded snatches of conversation that typically have provided some researcher with his or her data, but the articulate opinion of those African-American students who face the task of public school language education. It is not being idealistic to expect at least some students to be able to furnish such information if encouraged to do so. One would not expect the elaborate speculation that a writer such as Smitherman can provide but, nonetheless, much valuable knowledge could be gathered. I know that I, had I been asked in, say, 1964, could have told someone something about this clash between cultures, this problem of being Black and attempting to cope with the instruction offered in a school controlled by those of another background. But of course I was never asked by anyone in authority to speak about the conflict. I was just asked to survive it.

Years later, in 1979, I finally got around to discussing that earlier period. Between jobs and (though I didn't know it at the time) careers, with my first child on the way, I decided to fashion a gift of experience, of my education. I became obsessed with beginning to organize the things

I would need to say as a father. In tune with many prospective parents I planned to be "hard" on my child, but I also wanted things to be easier for him or her than they were for me.

I began to write a story of my life. Although I changed certain names and locations (freeing up my composing process), the writing is still undeniably autobiographical, as most long-term acquaintances of mine can attest. Despite working at breakneck pace, I had only completed the eighth grade again when Kahlil, a seven-pound, fifteen-ounce manchild, burst upon the scene. The text remained that way until I was later persuaded to add more.

As I reviewed my writing during the weeks following Kahlil's birth, I viewed the manuscript, entitled *Primary School*, as a story of educational survival cast mainly in racial terms. Only later, after I had become an English instructor and graduate student of sociolinguistics, did the realization set in that I had spun much of my record, developed that very theme of survival, around the acquisition and mastery of various communicative competencies. That survival, race consciousness, and communicative skill form a conceptual triangle in that writing is now very interesting to me, but not surprising. Wasn't it communication skill that brought the manuscript itself into existence? Wasn't the acute exercise of it my chief response to the stress I felt of welcoming a child into a world filled with race-related perils?

In 1980 I became an English teacher. On the college level I have worked with Black students who, for the most part, have been ill-prepared by the public schools to write the Standard English demanded of them. So while it has been an immediate responsibility to instruct the students in my basic writing courses the best I can, I feel that prevention in education is worth, at the very least, one ton of cure and, as such, I am concerned with language pedagogy along the full length of the curriculum. I have plunged into the sea of theoretical controversy described above, choosing to swim alongside those who see the legitimacy of Black verbal expression in formal educational contexts. My interest is not merely in the ways Black students can learn; I am also concerned about the psychic costs they pay. A pedagogy is successful only if it makes knowledge or skill achievable while at the same time allowing students to maintain their own sense of identity.

I have chosen to write about the various voices I have come to possess, to speak of my own psychic payments. Using my autobiographical narrative (the even-numbered chapters of this book) as a focal point, I have explored how I, as a native Black English speaker in an urban public school environment, acquired Standard English language skills. In addition I have addressed the broader subject of what was involved in acquiring certain strategies beyond strictly linguistic skills, namely mainstream *sociolinguistic competence*, which I employed in order to be a successful participant in certain settings. Such ability involves, as Philips (1972) suggests, "knowledge of when and in what style one must present one's utterances" (p. 372).

I developed my analytic approach out of the beliefs that, first, autobiographical artifacts serve as fairly accurate historical documents and, second, that human behavior is sensibly studied within the framework of a *transactional* model. I will elaborate on these two conceptions below.

An autobiographical account, despite its subjectivity, provides an important record of events the author has responded to — in short, what has shaped him or her as a social being. In a quest for such significance, the chronological facts of an individual's existence are not nearly as important as the psychological facts of forging a life, something autobiographies reveal quite well. Analysis of details presented in my autobiographical narrative, therefore, is crucial to an adequate understanding of my sociolinguistic development.

Although the personal narrative has been the primary data base, I have scrutinized my accumulated school record obtained from the Board of Education of the City of New York. Several documents appear in the Appendix of this volume. This step was not taken for the purposes of corroboration in any strict sense. The intent was to elaborate on the personal narrative — not to confirm it.

Eisner (1981) also addresses this issue:

> In artistic approaches to research, the cannons of test reliability and sampling do not apply. While one might consider or question a writer's or film producer's reliability, there is no formalized set of procedures to measure writer reliability; one doesn't really want the mean view of four writer's observations about the mental hospital in Oregon which served as the subject-matter for Ken Kesey's play [*One Flew Over The Cuckoo's Nest*]. One simply wants Ken Kesey's view. Its validity, if that is the appropriate term, is to be determined by our view of its credibility, and not by reducing his work to some average by using only that portion that it shares with the views of others. Validity in the arts is the product of the persuasiveness of a personal vision; its utility is determined by the extent to which it informs. There is no test of statistical significance, no measure of construct validity in artistically rendered research. What one seeks is illumination and penetration. The proof of the pudding is the way in which it shapes our conception of the world or some aspect of it. (p. 6)

Once I became convinced that my personal narrative was legitimate subject matter for a study of language development, I sought to specify social-psychological and linguistic principles that would guide my probing. In this light a transactional model, in which humans are viewed as continually negotiating with an evolving environment, appeared attractive. From this perspective, behavior is neither the exclusive acting out of inner drives, nor is it shaped solely by external forces. One has personal traits and a belief system that set one's expectations and guide one's actions. The results of these actions in turn modify that belief system. The modified belief system governs further action and so on. Such a model of human action is described in the work of George A. Kelly (1963). He terms it the *psychology of personal constructs*. In examining the data, I have not restricted myself to a consideration of my past sociolinguistic performances in and of themselves; rather, I have tried to determine the conceptions I held that caused me to perform as I did.

Noam Chomsky's viewpoint is similar (1957, 1972). He stresses that an active, scientific intellect lies at the center of the language acquisition process. Rather than merely absorbing and reproducing the speech surrounding them, children manipulate patterns and experiment with language choices as they come to grips with language on their own terms. I have evaluated the data from a compatible outlook, having related as far as possible my sociolinguistic development to my accompanying perception of self-interest.

This analysis of my autobiographical materials should prove useful to all those concerned with helping African-American students develop their ability to communicate in mainstream settings, for I have also dealt with issues of language pedagogy in more universal terms. This discussion is reported in chapters 3, 5, 7, and 9.

In chapter 3 I focus on language development up until the first grade. I inspect some of the differences between Black English and Standard English, and I indicate how code-switching develops as a communicative strategy. Reading theories and the growth of nonverbal skill also are considered.

Chapter 5 deals with linguistic and educational progress through the third grade. I look at how such progress, or lack thereof, may be affected by the social (with emphasis on race) climate of the school. My own progress is seen as the outcome of successful negotiation with classmates, school officials, family members, and community residents. I detail my response to educational proposals for dialect eradication, linguistic pluralism, and bidialectalism.

In chapter 7 I am concerned primarily with the relatively advanced self-concept students have formed by the close of elementary school. I demonstrate ways in which linguistic ability, societal awareness, political events, and various demands by peers may relate to that sense of self. Additionally, I explore how both the willingness and reluctance to code-switch on the part of students may cause problems for teachers and researchers.

Chapter 9, the conclusion, is not a mere summary of results. It mostly pertains to my journey through high school, my reflections on that passage, and the way in which that experience helped to shape my views on language education.

None of the issues raised in this book are original areas for investigation, nor is this work intended to be unique in that sense. I sought to present an account that will further illuminate matters for those involved with the education of African-American students. The noted anthropologist, Clifford Geertz (1973), conveys the spirit intended here:

> The essential vocation of interpretive anthropology is not to answer our deepest questions, but to make available to us answers that others, guarding other sheep in other valleys, have given, and thus to include them in the consultable record of what man has said. (p. 30)

2

First Lessons

Some events come before the memory. Completely beyond the veil of vagueness. Just no way to recall. The only knowledge I have of the times came through eavesdropping. I could not deal with direct questioning because it was clear that made me a bug. Try to open up the past and I would get shrugged off with stares like roach spray. So I just kept listening and observing and drawing my own conclusions, trying to get a sense of what the pre-memory was all about. That's important to me because it's a part of life too and it's a lot like the wind, you know, you can't see it but it can kick your rump pretty good if it blows hard enough.

I hit the scene uptown in 1952 on a Sunday afternoon. I think I started out as a good reason for all to be happy, but there was a curious error on the take-home copy of my birth certificate. In the space where the name of the father belongs my own name was written in. His was left off the document altogether. That error, however committed, was my first omen.

I hadn't yet cut a tooth when I received omen number two. A fire broke out in our apartment. Started in back of the refrigerator. My mother detected it first, yanked my one-year-old sister out of her bed, snatched me up from the crib, and hustled on outdoors. She didn't bother to arouse her husband/my dad. It's a blessing he managed to get out on his own. I've always thought that was a horrible thing for her to do although by the time I heard the story, with the influence I was under, I felt he probably deserved it. And I have chuckled about the event on numerous occasions since. But at other times I have pictured my father lying dead in a robe of bright yellow flames and felt my own palms moisten with fear. There was no doubt something cruel going on in our little world.

The signs persisted like ragweed. Sad events that would be revealed to me in tale. The tale of the perfectly thrown frying pan, you know, it's more feistiness than I would like to see in a woman of mine. Sherry and I were, in one sense, beneath it all. Down on the floor knocking over and spilling everything. But we also assumed a role in the power play as it was we who became its center. Mama took that battle also; as far back as we can remember we had the distinct impression that we belonged to her exclusively. We were her objects of adornment and possession, always dressed for compliments. Pops could get no primary billing in that setup. When I think back now to my earliest remembrances I sense him only as a haze in the background. And even as I reel forward again and he begins to crystallize for me, it's quite some time before he appears essential. Moms, on the other hand, was ranked up there next to sunlight from the beginning.

That's a long way to come from Ashford, Alabama. Way down by the Chipola River. Little Margie, with stubbornness her most celebrated trait. Might as well whip a tree, they would say, if you were figuring on whipping her for a confession. At least you spare your own self some pain. And she was real close to her few chosen friends. If she liked you she could bring you loyalty in a million wheelbarrows. Labeled "good potential," she worked far below it. Skated her way through school. Folks have camped just outside her earshot for years whispering, "She's smart so she could do better if. . . . "

Ammaziah, though bright, didn't have a chance to skate through school. He had to work on a farm northeast of Ashford, going up toward the Chattahoochee. "He's just a plain nice man" is the worst thing I have ever heard anybody outside of our own household say about him. And I guess it would be hard not to like a big and gentle Baptist with a basic decency who could hold his liquor and had a name you could make fun of.

He liked to watch all the horses run and all the New York women too. Couldn't lick either gamble. He hadn't developed enough finesse for the big town. I know he tried hard at times but whenever he put together two really good steps irresponsibility would rear up and knock him back three. He couldn't be any Gibraltar for you.

All this going on around our heads. The big folks. Both destined to be enshrined in the best-friend-you-could-possibly-have hall of fame, provided they could keep each other off the selection committee. But they still hung out together. Hadn't fully understood the peace that can crop up here and there amid the greatest confusion. And right in the middle of 1954 came daughter number two. Judy ate well and slept a lot, then less, and grew to be a good partner to knock around with as we caromed off the walls of the Harlem flat and tumbled forward.

In the early reaches of memory events swirl about like batches of stirred leaves. No order or sequence. I remember we had two pet turtles. One had a yellow shell. The other's was red. We kept them in a bowl with a little plastic palm tree and tiny cream-colored pebbles. Sherry fed them and I poured in the fresh water. Well the turtles were a bit frisky. They often climbed out of the bowl and we had to overturn tables and cushions and chairs to find them. I don't recall how many times we went on this chase but it was all over one morning when they were found under the sofa with their bellies ripped open by rats. For a long time afterward I would associate rats with turtlemeat first, rather than cheese, which I guess isn't exactly a good start toward a high IQ.

So the turtles died early on. But I can't tell you whether that was before the back of my head was split open on the front stoop. There was a bunch of us out there preparing to run a dash down 146th Street. Victory wasn't the main thing in these races. Just please don't come in last or you would be the first one to get your mother talked about and everything. I had poor position inside along the rail next to this chubby girl, but as we came thundering past the front of the building I began to pull away from her. I was getting away from the last spot for sure when she reached out and pushed me down. My head banged hard into the edge of a concrete step and the blood started dripping down the back of my neck and I started screaming like crazy. Then I had to get shaven bald in one spot and look like a jerk so I could get patched up right. But that was better still than being last. I mean I had heard Pee Wee Thomas, who was in school already, tell Tyrone that the reason he was so slow was because whoever Tyrone's father was had to be slow too not to have been able to get away from Tyrone's ugly damn mama.

There was a babysitter we went to sometimes down on Seventh Avenue. Her name was Janine and she had boy-girl twins, Diane and Darnell, who were a few months older than Sherry. She was real nice and let us drag our toys all over the house, but whenever her husband, Butch, would come home early in the afternoon she would round us up quickly and herd us into the kids' room. We were under strict orders not to come out and of course we didn't. But she never said anything about peeping. The first time was at Darnell's suggestion. We crept up to the door and cracked it with the stealth of cat burglars. I couldn't see over Sherry and the twins so I crouched to the floor and never did get a look at the action. Darnell almost burst out laughing and we retreated to the farthest corner of the room. We sent Judy off to play with some blocks.

"What is they doin Sherry?" I whispered as I took a seat atop Darnell's wagon.

"Oh you so stupid Keith."

"Well I ain't see so good."

"Oh you just so stupid. Tell him Darnell." She and Diane were giggling.

"No you Sherry."

"No Darnell you."

"It's your brother. You 'pose to."

"I can't. I don't know for real."

"You know for real."

"No I don't."

"Then why you laughin?"

"I was laughin at you." And they all started laughing at each other. Then Darnell came and whispered in my ear: "They doin nasty."

"NASTY OOOOH NAS —." Darnell clamped his hand over my mouth. "You gotta be quiet Keith or we can't go no more."

I was quiet. And got to go many times before I decided, or was it Diane who decided, that we could do some nasty of our own. But we announced our intentions first and Sherry squealed and Janine gave both of us a spanking. Barely five, I was mad I had to wait.

I remember one Saturday we were coming home from the beauty parlor with my mother. I had on my cowboy get up, six-shooters at my sides. We were walking well up in front of her as usual, trained to stop at the corner. That morning, however, I took it into my head to go dashing across Eighth Avenue on my own. I think I saw my father but I'm not sure. I know I didn't look for any traffic lights. I tripped about halfway across and couldn't get to my feet again. I was struggling hard but my coordination had deserted me. Like scrambling on ice. There was a screeching of brakes and then the most gigantic bus imaginable was hovering over me. I still couldn't get the feet to work together. I was somehow yanked from under the bus, dragged the rest of the way across the street and, with my own pistols, beaten all the way up the block. It was a fierce thrashing and there were folks out there imploring my mother to stop. But verbal support was all I received. Wasn't anybody out there going to risk tangling with Moms. I have never fallen in any roadway, nor been pistol-whipped, since.

One evening we were digging into some fruit cocktail after dinner and heard a great ruckus out in the hallway. The cops were chasing these two drug addicts and they were headed for the roof. "They's junkies I know" said a man across the hall. Sherry had mentioned something about junkies to me before, but when the police paraded them down the stairs stark naked with their hands cuffed behind their backs it was the first time I had a good opportunity to see what they actually looked like. It was somewhat disappointing, however, for they looked just about like everybody else.

I was bringing a loaf of bread home from the store when I saw this gray dog getting his neck chewed off in a dogfight on the corner. I dropped my bag to go save him and was trying to push my way through the circle of gamblers and spectators when this huge man hoisted me up onto his shoulder. He thought I merely wanted a better view. Before I could figure a way to get down another man rescued the dog, though he was cursing the poor animal, and green bills changed hands around the circle.

Sherry had gone off to kindergarten and I decided to give Judy a sex change operation while our mother was asleep. I slipped her into a change of my clothing as I kept reassuring her. "You know it gon be more fun. You know it right?" She was properly willing. We had to roll the pants up at the bottom and her feet couldn't make it down into the toes of my sneakers but we could live with that. But we were dissatisfied with her hair. Such soft long braids. Boys get away with that now but not in '57.

"You gotta cut it."

"Then I be a boy Keith? I finish that I be a boy?"

"Yeah you'll be one. It gon be more fun too."

Scissors please. She wouldn't cut it in one fell swoop like I wanted her to do. She started nibbling at the edges. Tiny dark patches falling gently to the floor. As she became more relaxed, however, she began to clip at a faster pace and made a clearing on one side all the way to the scalp. I was urging her to clip even faster, "go head Judy go head," when Sherry came charging into the apartment, saw what was taking place, let out a long and soulful "Oooooooooh I'm gonna tell Ma," and ran into the other room to awaken her. I began to sweat.

"You made me" Judy accused.

"No I didn't and you gon git in trouble and git a beatin too."

"You made me."

"I did not."

"Yes you did."

"I DID NOT." I had to get loud to prove my innocence. Moms was already approaching fast like an enraged lioness and I wanted no part of her fury. She slashed me across the legs with her strap and cast me aside. I was getting off light. Unbelievably so. But Judy got it all.

Maybe I could have stood up for Judy, but by then I was taking the

vast majority of the whippings in the household. So I guess I figured what
the heck, Judy could stand to share some of the weight. She may have
become a trifle less eager to pursue my ideas of fun but I was sort of growing bored with running around the house with her all morning anyway.
I mean Sherry was bringing home books and fingerpaintings all the time
and making kindergarten seem like the hip thing.

It was all right I suppose. Artwork and musical chairs and fairy tales.
The biggest kindergarten thrill for me, however, was the chance to come
home along Eighth Avenue unescorted. Sherry didn't get out until three
o'clock and my mother didn't embarrass me by picking me up like I was
a baby, so every day I had a three-and-a-half-block distance to negotiate
as I pleased. Or at least I took it that way.

Some of us would go scampering along the Avenue. Anything could
happen out there. The side streets were tall and narrow with hallways no
more interesting than our own. But Eighth Avenue, well, that was the real
world. We stuck our noses into the barber shop, the shoe repair shop, the
fish market, the bars. The conversation was mostly baseball and whores.
Willie Mays was clearly the Prince of Uptown, and the next best thing
you could be was a pimp. We threw stones at sleeping winos and followed
the vegetable wagon all the way down to 140th Street waiting for the
horse to move his bowels in the middle of the street. Then we'd stay and
watch the cars run over the large piles of dung. Every time a tire scored
a bull's eye we'd shout "Squish" and spin about with glee. Don't let it be
a truck that scored. Ecstasy. Sometimes we would run straight across
148th Street to Colonial Park to play tag and rock fight and climb the hill
until the guilt snuck up on us one by one and then, each according to his
conscience, we would begin to head for home.

From the very beginning my mother couldn't understand why it should
take me over an hour to walk less than four blocks, especially when it
meant showing up with my new jacket all muddy or my pants ripped at
the knee, you know, the kinds of things you never notice until your mother
points them out. And she made all her points clear with that belt. I tried
telling her that the clock on the kitchen wall must be broken or something
because I always ran straight home, but she wouldn't buy it. I eventually
had to come around. And that's when I really got jammed.

There was a substitute teacher for our class one day and she didn't
know the proper time to dismiss us. It must have been going on 12:30 and
she was still reading us a story about Curious George. Our class was at
the end of the hall, so when the other classes let out we couldn't hear
them. There was no impatient parent to rescue us. The substitute just kept
on and on about this wonderful monkey.

Finally she sensed something was wrong and asked us what time we were supposed to let out.

"Twelve o'clock" we chorused.

"Oh no" she exclaimed. "Are you sure?"

"We get out twelve o'clock" some of us repeated, as general chatter erupted about the room. Louis went up to her and said, "We get out when the two hands is straight up. That's twelve o'clock right?" She ran out of the room. When she returned a few moments later she was shouting "Hats and coats everybody. Hats and coats now. We're late."

Late was the last word I needed to hear. She couldn't let us out of there fast enough to suit me. I sprinted home as swiftly as possible, scaled the six flights of stairs in record time, and as I burst into the apartment out of breath my mother, as I knew she would be, was waiting for me belt in hand. She backed me up against the door with her stern voice.

"Haven't I told you about not coming straight home from school?" I caught my breath. I was sure glad I was armed with the truth.

"Ma we had a substitute. We had a substitute Ma and she didn't know what time to let us out. I ran all the way home."

"Boy don't tell that barefaced lie. I'll take the skin off your backside for lyin to me."

"But I ain't lyin Ma. I ain't.

"Shut up boy! Ain't no teacher can keep no class late like that."

"But she was readin us a story."

"Shut up I said. Don't be standin there and givin me no cold-ass argument." She drew back the strap and I cringed in terror. I sidestepped her, as the first blow crashed against my thigh, and took off for the living room. She was right behind me. I dove to my knees and stuck my head under the couch. It was one of the several defensive maneuvers I had developed by then. I was always mortgaging my rear to save my head. Wasn't going to let anybody beat me in the head. Which was all right with Moms.

"You ain't accomplishin nothing by stickin that behind up there like that boy. That's the part I want any old how. I'll teach you yet about not payin me no mind." She had that talking-beating rhythm in high gear. You know how you had to receive a lecture to go along with your whipping. And can't anyone on earth hand out a more artistic ass whipping than a Black woman can. Syncopated whippings: Boy didn't I lash lash tell you about lash lash lying to me? Lash lash lash lash hunh? Lash hunh boy? Lash lash lash hunh boy? Hunh? I was always supposed to answer these questions although my answering them never stopped anything and sometimes made matters worse, especially if I was giving the wrong answers as I was that day. Although I was hollering my head off I still managed to insist upon my innocence. To no avail. Lash lash lash I will break your behind lash if necessary lash boy. Do you hear me? Do you lash lash hear me?

I heard and I felt and it hurt both ways. After the beating I continued to proclaim my innocence. Only stopped when she became angry all over again and threatened me with more punishment. Afterwards I complained to my sisters on occasion, but it was weeks before I mentioned the incident to my mother again. She just gave me a warm smile and said, "I'll tell you something Keith. It all evens out."

Sibling rivalry stalked me from behind. I was getting intensive reading lessons from Sherry and had made progress to the point where I was ready to show off for Moms. We had her cornered on the sofa and I was holding the book out in front of me. Sherry was on my right, ready to help if I faltered, so I started reading something like:

> "See here," said Don. "Here are blue flowers. We want blue flowers. Let us get blue flowers."

It was something along those lines, you know, and I was performing well. My mother was beaming and I had her undivided attention until Judy came out of somewhere, slid the edge of a razor blade into the side of my face clear to the bone, narrowly missing my eye, and ripped a deep diagonal clean past my ear.

Blood popped out everywhere. I spent what seemed like hours with my head ducked under a running faucet. Towels. Compresses. Mercurochrome. Bandages. Then my mother seized a high-heeled shoe and beat Judy worse than she had beaten me for almost getting myself killed out on the Avenue.

My little sister never apologized. In fact she used to taunt me about this incident as she was later becoming a favorite target for my aggression. No matter what I did to her. Kick her, trip her, whatever. She would just keep repeating, "So I cut you in the face."

"Do it again" I would retort most angrily.

"I did it already."

"I dare you to do it again. I'll push you out the window."

"No you won't."

"Yes I will."

"No you won't."

"I will so."

"Then I'll cut you in your face again."

"Then come on. Come on if you still think you so big and bad."

"I ain't scared."

"Come on then sucker."

"I'll cut you right in the face again."

"What you waitin for then fraidy cat?"

"I did it already."

She was about as mean a three year old as you will ever find.

Actually I had my hardest battles with Sherry. She was good for teaching me things but when her mood shifted I had to watch out. She gave me my next permanent scar by pressing a hot steam iron to the back of my hand. Burned off a circle of flesh. I later shattered a light bulb against the bridge of her nose but she escaped unharmed. I think you can say we were taking this rivalry thing a bit too seriously.

At times my sisters would double-team me. We were heavily into words now and when my sisters discovered that to stifle mine was the best weapon they could use against me, it led to some of the unhappiest moments I can recall. They had found my fledgling sensitivity, clutched it about the windpipe, and squeezed. They teased me and baited me but whenever I began to reply they would shout as loudly as they could to obscure what I was saying. Their favorite lines were "Am sam sam sam sam. Am sam sam sam sam." As soon as I parted my lips they would start chanting and send me straight to tears. I would wipe aside the water, swallow hard to compose myself, and fall apart all over again. I could rumble and accept insults but I couldn't ever deal with not being allowed to speak. Their am sam curse was too devastating. I had neither the sense to ignore nor the strength to attack.

I don't recall much about a whole pregnancy, but when my mother left for the hospital one night in June of '58 there was only a single wish ringing in my consciousness: BOY. And I knew I would get a brother because it was the only thing that could even the score. He would be my guarantee to be heard because wasn't anybody going to brainwash little brother but me. I alone would teach him how to bound down the stairs two at a time and sneak to the park. And he'd be the real thing. No imitation like Judy. No turncoat like Sherry. I knew I would have to handle his fights for him but that was fine as long as he listened to me and helped me beat the am sam curse. We'd start our own "Ooma booma booma booma" or something like that. Fix them good.

When the phone rang my grandmother, who was up from Alabama, reached it first. I watched her smile as she spoke. As she turned toward me she was saying, "Yeah he standin right here. You know he can't wait to hear the news." She handed me the receiver.

"Hi Ma."

"Hi" she answered dreamily. "You finally have another sister."

I was condemned. I dropped the receiver and walked out of the room in a daze. Debra Lynn showed up a few days later with a head full of wild hair. She was a beauty, and from that day to this she has never been out of my heart. But she couldn't be a brother.

I had just one more summer to pass on 146th Street. Farmer Gray cartoons in the morning. The Jocko Show in the afternoon. Sit down and rock Debra Lynn for a spell or jump up and go wild to the rhythm of my first favorite record, "Tequila," by the Champs. And I was beginning to tread more lightly about the apartment, trying to avoid all scars and bruised feelings, overjoyed at any opportunity to go outside. Just give me the playground or send me to the corner grocery so I can squeeze in as much Eighth Avenue as possible before I have to hurry back. I couldn't shoot a basketball high enough to make a goal but I began learning how to dribble and saw my first pair of dead wide open eyes on a fat man lying amid a crowd in front of the fish market with a thin jagged line of blood across the width of his throat.

On Sundays, for religion, we went up on the hill. Skipping along the hexagon-shaped tile in Colonial Park. Darting up the steps to Edgecomb Avenue. Stopping in the candy store on St. Nicholas to load up. Leaning forward for leverage to finish the climb up to the church. I was always impressed by this particular house of the Lord. Tremendous gray and white cinder blocks. Polished maple pews in the main service room. Red carpet, stained windows, and gigantic organ pipes. And the Lord, he owned the best singers available. There was nothing like a gorgeous soprano wailing and sweating under influence of the spirit and a hot wig. There were always old women with blue dye in their hair shrieking and swooning during the sermon as folks around them grabbed hold of them while exclaiming, "Yes Lord. I see you done come to us." With women like that falling out in droves you had to believe. And Pops was up in the front row with the rest of the deacons. A broad-shouldered frame in a gray or blue suit. Sometimes wore white gloves to serve communion. He always winked at us when he passed by.

The first grade brought a teacher, Miss Novick, who we thought was the top genius on the planet. She was going to turn us all into little scientists she would say. And there was invariably one experiment or another for us to observe.

She placed a glass jar, two small candles in holders, and a box of matches on her desk. She raised the jar and candles over her head and waved them slowly for all to see.

"I have here a glass jar and two simple candles. Can everyone see them?"

"Yes Miss Novick" we replied, speaking as everyone.

"See them James?"

"Yeah."

"See them Karen?"

"Uh hunh."

"See them John?"

"I sees it."

"Okay." She returned the objects to her desk, lit the candles and held them overhead. Our eyes were transfixed with magic show expectations.

"Now the candles are lit. You see? Rosanne? Ryan? Keith?" I gave a nod of affirmation. Then she lowered the candles to the desk and lifted the jar, upside down, as we inched forward in our seats.

"Now who can tell me what will happen if I set this jar down over one of these flames? Can anyone tell me? James?" He could not. He was smart but stumped. Sat looking dumb with his face greased and his eyes bulged and his index finger glued to his chin.

"How about you Barbara?"

"You gonna catch the des' on fire Miss Novick."

"YEAAHHHHHHHHH. . . . "

"No, little scientists. No. No. No. We will not harm the desk. Anyone else? . . . No? . . . Well let us observe."

She placed the jar over one of the candles and we stared eagerly at both flames until the one inside the jar died out. Miss Novick surveyed our puzzled faces and smiled.

"Now why did that happen class?"

"You mean why it went out?"

"Yes Harold. Can you tell me why?"

"Because you put that jar on there. You made it go out Miss Novick. You did it."

"Sure Harold. But how could I do it with only the jar?"

"I don't know. Was there some water in there?"

"There wasn't Harold. We all looked at the jar together, remember?"

"Oh yeah."

"Anyone else?" Miss Novick was extremely patient and thoroughly flustered us all before giving us our first formal explanation concerning oxygen.

I liked the prospect of becoming a resident scientist up at P.S. 90 (strange what faith I had in the public school system up there), and when the announcement came later that fall that we were moving into a house out in Queens I was, at first, a bit disheartened. I knew there were scientific experiments elsewhere but I wasn't so sure I could get another Miss Novick or even more important, in a related field, another Eighth Avenue.

I wasn't anti-Queens; all I knew about the place was that it was over a bridge somewhere. But I surely had no beef with Harlem. I didn't recoil at the sight of its streets as I would at other times later in life. I had no sense of society being so terrible. I was there and I fit.

On another level, however, I guess I did welcome a chance to leave the apartment I was associating more and more with misunderstanding and pain. *House* sounded like more space to stay out of the way of others.

So at the age of six it was time for a crossing. My young mind poised for any game that came along. Could play the middle or skirt the fringe as I saw fit. Just come out stepping light and easy, you know, and if it gets hectic remember to cover in the clinch. The point was to hold the defense together while all about me from complex fabrics of frustration and rejection and sensitivity and conflict and hope and loneliness and resignation and reticence and wonderment and bewilderment and romantic notions and romantic disappointments, from all this and more, the imposing offense was being woven.

And the bridge bowed gracefully and beckoned. Bore me upon its majestic back and arched me high above the cold and swirling dark waters of that November toward another shore, and another truth, which all should know: Most times a bridge is just another two-way street.

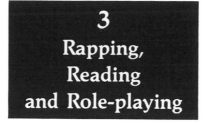

3
Rapping, Reading and Role-playing

Early Language

The speech of a large group of African-Americans has been given many labels, including Ebonics, Black English Vernacular, and just plain Black English. The last term is by far the most popular. I will use it throughout this text to refer to my native tongue, that is, the language variety I first acquired and the one I have always been able to use with greatest facility.

The idea of Black English is still controversial despite research dating back three decades, which documents that it is a legitimate linguistic system and not merely a collection of verbal aberrations arrived at by the reckless violation of the rules of a so-called superior variety of English. But let us presently make an end run around that debate. The intent here is not to argue the existence or overall merits of Black English. The case has been made quite well by scholars such as Smitherman (1977), Dillard (1973), and Haskins and Butts (1973). The most pressing purpose at this point is to demonstrate how the dialogue of the Keith character (me) is reflective of that language variety.* The analysis is meant to be indicative rather than exhaustive. As such, a thorough review of the rules of Black English will not be required. Structural explanations will be offered only to further illuminate the specific portions of the text being considered. Perhaps it is instructive, however, to include a general definition. Smitherman's should suffice: "Black Dialect is an Africanized form of English re-

---

*Again, the premise is that these sequences, while not actual, are certainly plausible.

flecting Black America's linguistic-cultural heritage and the conditions of servitude, oppression and life in America" (p. 2).

In the previous chapter, as the four youngsters are engaged in the Peeping Tom scene, we find the following snatches of dialogue.

> (1) "What is they doin Sherry?" (Keith speaking)
> (2) "Oh you so stupid Keith." (Sherry speaking)
> (3) "Then why you laughin?" (Darnell speaking)
> (4) "They doin nasty." (Darnell speaking)

The *is they* combination in sentence 1 would be identified as an error in noun-verb agreement under the rules of Standard English; however, this construction exemplifies the Black English convention of simplifying the conjugation of the verb *to be*. Smitherman again explains: "When the forms of *be* are used, they are simplified so that *is* and *was* usually serve for all subjects of sentences, whether the subjects are singular or plural, or refer to *I*, *you*, *we* or whatever" (p. 21).

Skeptics may suggest that this speech is not an example of some Black English rule but simply the utterance of a child who has yet to master this element of agreement. After all, the speaker in this case is only five, an age at which noun-verb agreement errors are likely still to be numerous for any speaker of English. However, I must counter that the type of noun-verb error committed by a five year old in the process of acquiring Standard English is of a different nature than constructions like *is they*. Consider the description by Beck (1979) of the language of the five- to six-year old child relative to noun-verb combinations:

> The child should be advancing in use of the full verb system, although errors, particularly in noun and verb number agreement, are still prevalent. . . . The kindergarten child is as likely to say "There is flowers" as to say "There are flowers," the head word sounding singular to the child, who incorrectly anticipates the major noun's number. (p. 96)

The puzzlement that exists for the child in Beck's presentation is not to be found in the case of *is they* or, by transformation to the declarative form, *they is*. Here there is no question that the noun, *they*, is plural. The choice of the accompanying verb, *is*, is definitely not based on a perception of singularity as opposed to plurality and thus cannot be said to epitomize number confusion. Furthermore, and a more obvious rebuttal, I made *they is* "mistakes" long past the age that the speaker of strictly Standard English eventually masters even the most difficult aspects of noun-verb agreement. In fact, I am still making them. But my *they is* type of talk is not merely a transitory stage in the acquisition of Standard English. It clearly points to a deeply held rule, one I already was adhering to at the age of five. The simplification of the verb *to be*, like several other features of Black English, can only erroneously be viewed as representing a stage, or worse, an arrest in the acquisition of an alternate linguistic system.

Operative in sentences 2, 3, and 4 is the much discussed zero copula rule, that is, the omission of *be* when it would only refer to events fixed in time and nonrepeating (Smitherman, p. 21). Thus we get in sentence 2 *you so* and not *you are so*; in 3, *why you* and not *why are you*; in 4, *they doin* and not *they are doin*. Although these lines are not exact quotations, it is obvious that, as a member of that peer group, I produced these types of utterances. This is not, by the way, to suggest that language learning is solely an imitative activity. We understand from Kelly (1963) that the essential nature of human learning lies not in imitating but in active construing. Fortunately, I speak so many zero copula phrases, both real and literary, that the claim above does not have to be based solely on the evidence so far chosen. I have opted to make the case at this juncture for purposes of organization.

Let us look at sentence 1 from another angle. Although the speaker of *is they* conforms to a rule of Black English, he ignores the zero copula rule, which he also uses on occasion. The zero copula rule is a non-obligatory rule, whereas the simplification of *to be* is required. Put another way, one may use a form of *to be* and still be speaking Black English, but that form must be *is* or *was*. It is interesting enough to ponder why he chose to bypass the zero copula rule while his sister and friends were using it. But matters become even more intriguing when one is aware that yet another rule of Black English was bypassed, that of question formation. Questions in Black English can be asked by means of rising intonation (Burling 1973). Thus one could hear "What they is doin?" as well as "What is they doin?" So the issue now is to determine what significance can be attached to sentence 1 in light of the fact that it reflects two choices to ignore certain rules of Black English. More on this a little later.

In the haircut scene, there is a two-sentence response to an inquiry by Judy.

(5) "Yeah you'll be one."
(6) "It gon be more fun too."

Note the use of the auxiliary in sentence 5, *you'll*, while in 6 it is ignored (an instance of zero copula). Sentence 5 is not Black English at all, although we can discern from the grammar of the following sentence that the speaker surely had the ability to say, "Yeah you gon be one." The contrast is even greater than that spotted in the earlier dialogue. Also note that *gon* represents a strong Black English phonology pattern. The sound system of Black English is relatively difficult to capture in print, but the contraction *gon* in place of *going to* is, nevertheless, a stark indicator. Smitherman describes its formation: "Here the *to* is omitted altogether, and the nasal sound at the end is shortened, producing a sound that is somewhat like an abbreviated form of *gone*" (p. 18). To reiterate though, this option was not chosen in Sentence 5.

In the whipping scene, we see that the mother initiates the dialogue with a question that is clearly Standard English. The reply is equally standard. But when the story is flatly rejected and the physical threat becomes immediate, whatever coolness has been maintained gives way and the dialect changes.

(7) "Boy don't tell that barefaced lie."
(8) "I'll take the skin off your backside for lyin to me."
(9) "But I ain't lyin Ma."
(10) "I ain't."

In part the child, in sentences 9 and 10, is following the lead of his mother who not only has added to his stress but has actually shifted, in 7 and 8, into an alternate vernacular. Great variance in grammatical structure is not apparent in this speech, nor is the huge phonological shift evident. However, the semantics are telling. This is clearly the talk of Black folks. And it is not at all surprising that very quickly we come across a multiple (triple or more) negation.

(11) "Ain't no teacher can keep no class late like that."

This pattern of negation, distinct from the double negatives that appear commonly in all nonstandard forms of English, occurs quite frequently in Black English and is perhaps the most noncontroversial marker of that language variety.

My mother is a bidialectal speaker, capable of producing Black English and Standard English as well. And it should be obvious, with the examples so far adduced, that even in the preschool years my own move toward bidialectalism was well underway, made possible no doubt by my awareness of my mother's verbal maneuvering. I had seen how she could speak to a grocer, a salesman, a doctor, or a stranger in one manner (Standard), and then turn around, watch me carelessly knock a bowl of cereal on the floor, and exclaim, "Now look what you done did!" She was displaying and I was learning a technique linguists refer to as code-switching. Elgin (1979) defines this phenomenon as the "ability to move back and forth among languages, dialects, and registers with ease, as demanded by the social situation" (p. 109). Although this is a pretty fair description of the skill involved, the word *ease* is objectionable as it seems to imply that the whole process is somehow psychically neat. I have often chosen to switch, rather than fight, but the routine hasn't always implied any emotional ease. For a definition that is essentially similar yet allows the appropriate room for pain, one may consult Penalosa (1981). He defines code-switching as "a strategy by which the skillful speaker uses his knowledge of how language choices are interpreted in his community to structure the interaction so as to maximize outcomes favorable to himself" (p. 77).

That my mother was the chief agent helping me to learn to code-switch should not raise any eyebrows. She was, after all, the dominant person in my life. There appears, however, to have been some specific sociolinguistic principle operative as well. Labov (1981) contends that women generally employ more prestige forms than men and tend to exhibit much greater fluctuation in the modes they employ. The fact that my mother achieved the status of number-one role model for bidialectal speech patterns in both the text and in my present recollection was only, as Labov indicates, the most likely outcome.

Despite this discussion of bidialectalism, bear in mind that such discourse does no damage to the claim that Black English is my native tongue. It merely demonstrates that I was not growing up as a speaker of the basilect or most uncontaminated form of the language (see Stewart 1969). Relatively few Blacks are. A child, indeed a whole community, would have to exist in extreme isolation for any language variety to remain pure. I would expect, therefore, most Blacks to be bidialectal to some extent. But if we accept another contention of Labov, that no one is ever perfectly bidialectal, that is, even-handed in a linguistic sense, I think we can safely assert, based on the evidence then and now, that for me Black English was developing as the dominant tongue while Standard English, though quite significant, was not wielded as handily.

With this information to augment the text, we can return to the dialogue cited earlier and more firmly avow that it is authentic in that it captures the reality that forms of Standard English were also being acquired. What initially may seem to be blundering manipulations of voice are better understood as accurate portrayals of an emerging bidialectalism. To render the speech only in Black English would not have been genuine.

Therefore we should expect sentences like number 1. There is no doubt that this is Black English, but the use of the auxiliary *is* and its placement immediately preceding the subject, *they,* displays competence (subject-auxiliary inversion) in forming interrogatives along the lines of Standard English. Similarly, the use of *you'll* in sentence 5 manifests mastery of the contraction system. Beck indicates that both of these capabilities generally come to be distinct, indeed, in the speech of the five to six year old.

With this in mind, it should startle no one that sentence 6, a decidedly Black English sentence, follows sentence 5, for it highlights the juxtaposing of dialects that was occurring. Of great importance, in addition, is that each case of shifting or mixing happens as the child is experiencing conflicting social demands. In the Peeping Tom scene, he must appear knowledgeable even while being forced to ask a question of slightly older peers; the haircut scene requires that he talk down to a three year old yet coax her into action; and in the whipping scene, it is necessary that he try to inject some special combination of caution and urgency in his voice in an attempt to avoid physical punishment. This implies an awareness of the social relevance of dialects, a skill often assigned by scholars to a later stage of development. Smitherman, for example, indites that "among school-age blacks, one would find a greater degree of bi-dialectalism among older adolescents than among younger black children, for adolescents have begun to get hip to the social sensitivities associated with different kinds of languages and dialects" (pp. 31–32). I think folks get hip long before that age. The crucial dynamic is choice. Younger children, mostly out of self-defense, are not on the whole as willing to "play the game." But they can perceive much of the game and could play a lot of it if they so desired.

Troike (1972) asserts that even the youngest schoolchildren pay a great deal of attention to the social significance of dialect differences. Speaking of the child's ability to alternate between linguistic systems, he reasons that "despite cultural beliefs to the contary, even very young children are often quite aware of the social relevance of stylistic and dialect differences" (p. 305). He proceeds to give the example of a first-grader who was given a picture in a magazine and asked to tell a story about it to a researcher.

> The girl drew herself up, began "Once upon a time, . . . " and launched into a very formal narrative which was notable for containing no contractions. At the end of the story, she visibly relaxed, and from there on freely used contractions for the remainder of the interview. The whole subject of the range of styles and dialects in the productive and receptive repertory of children is only just beginning to receive attention, and a great deal yet remains

to be learned. Nevertheless, it is clear that even pre-first-graders are far from linguistically naive and have already learned a great deal about the adaptive significance of linguistic behavior within their own very real social world. (p. 309)

The whole question of the child's social awareness of dialect differences will be of major concern, of course, throughout this work. At present, the essential notion to understand is that this social awareness on my part was considerably sharpened even during the preschool years.

I carried with me a tremendously empowering repertoire of speaking and listening skills when I shuffled off to public school and continued to expand it once I arrived. Included in my bag of communicative tricks were that prize strategem, Black English, a productive (speaking) biloquialism, and a broader receptive (listening) bidialectalism. There was also an adroitness at responding to the perceived need to match each dialect to different sets of social circumstances. All this achievement may appear quite marvelous and, I guess, actually is. But it represents nothing miraculous beyond the basic miracle of existing, nothing special among Black children, nothing that should not be the case if a developing mind is pretty much left alone. Put more succinctly, it really ain't no new news.

Reading Acquisition

As the story indicates, I literally shed blood in the process of learning how to read. Such action should not become the basis for educational policy (though perhaps on a symbolic level it has), but it does indicate, in a way that only blood can, just how important I felt reading was. Being able to comprehend print allowed me to participate in my environment on yet another level; it was a skill I just had to have. Naturally, therefore, I kept close tabs on whatever progress my older sister was making toward literacy, and I was, in fact, doing a considerable amount of reading before I received any formal school instruction. (Such instruction could not have come before first grade, at which point I was already six and a half.)

I will attempt here to sketch how this reading acquisition transpired. First I will speak about the reading process in broad, general terms; then I will pay particular attention to the controversy that inevitably surrounds a discussion of initial reading instruction. I will consider then the role that literature (such as the fairy tales mentioned three times in the text) played in my personal attempts to read. And finally I will elaborate on the notion, alluded to above, of literacy in the context of social relations.

THE READING PROCESS

Frank Smith (1971, 1979) asserts that since there are no unique physical structures in the brain that specifically account for the ability to read, there is nothing special to say about reading once a correct assessment of human learning in general has been made (1979, p. 2). In his view, when we look at print we derive meaning from it in much the same way as we derive meaning from other objects in the world. We recognize it, which is an alternate way of saying that we reduce all our relevant uncertainty about what it is, and we make informed predictions as to its meaning, which rule out unlikely occurrences. Smith realizes that "prediction is not a new and artificial skill that has to be learned but the *natural* way to make sense of the world" (1979, p. 77). We will make mistakes of course, but the point is that the mistakes are insignificant if they don't interfere with actual meaning. Or as Smith himself asks, "If a mistake makes no difference, then what difference can it make?" (1979, p. 34). A fluent reader, he gathers, will probably bother with only one-fifth of the graphic information on the page.

Smith further argues that if one, in fact, tries to make too precise an identification of individual words or letters while reading, this increases his or her chance of error. By analogy he explains:

> The situation is rather similar for a sentry on duty on a dark night who hears approaching footsteps but who cannot reveal his own position by asking questions. His alternatives are to shoot or hold his fire. If he shoots and the intruder is indeed hostile, then the sentry will get a medal. If he holds his fire and the stranger is friendly his decision is also commendable. But a miss (letting through an enemy) or a false alarm (shooting a friend) are less desirable consequences. Yet the nature of the world is such that sentries always have to settle for some level of probability for the undesirable consequences; the man anxious to stop every enemy is going to shoot a friend from time to time, while the sentry anxious not to shoot a friend is occasionally going to let an enemy slip through. . . . The skilled reader cannot afford to set his criterion too high for deciding on word or meaning identification; we see that if he demands too much visual information, he will often be unable to get it fast enough to overcome memory limitations and read for sense. (1971, pp. 24–25)

Making sense, of course, is the single most important thing about reading, for it is the urge that motivates us to read in the first place. And within the limits of his general conception, which clearly argues the centrality of an anticipatory psychology to an understanding of the reading process, Smith offers several specific insights into the act of reading that merit attention here. First is that efficient readers do not decode to sound. If this were not so, if they did decode to sound, then they could read no faster than the rate of speech or the rate at which they could hear the words inside their heads. It is known that skilled readers (perhaps like yourself) can read several times faster than the average rate of speech. So Smith's stance appears to be correct. A related insight is that one cannot read one word at a time and read for sense. This is due, as alluded to above, to the physical limitations of short-term memory. If a person is reading at such a slow pace, he or she cannot hold enough strands of information in his or her brain simultaneously in order to make necessary connections, to make sense. A third belief that logically follows is that the most fluent readers are the ones who require the least visual information. And fourth is the notion that "meaningful language is transparent; we look through words for the meaning beyond" (1979, p. 123).

Some affirmation of Smith's approach can be found in the work of Isakson (1979). His research, in which the performances of college students on a reaction-time test were measured, indicates that sense is indeed extracted directly from print in meaning units as opposed to word units:

> The reader seems to be searching actively for the information which, combined with his general world knowledge, will allow him to identify the structural relationships between the words he has encountered. When the information is sufficient for at least a tentative identification of structure, processing activity increases so as to integrate the words received up to that point. (p. 164)

Kenneth Goodman (1967) has offered a view of the reading process, which he terms a "psycholinguistic guessing game," which also supports Smith's position. He specifically criticizes Spache (1964) and McCracken and Walcutt (1963) for having forwarded the notion of reading as a linear, cumulative process rather than as a selective leap toward meaning.

THE NOT-SO-GREAT DEBATE

Much has been made of the argument between those who favor a global (reading for meaning) approach to reading instruction and those who favor a code approach (usually phonics). Scholars of the Smith-Goodman ilk favor the global method of course. Their view is a logical extension of the theoretical stance described above. Let us consider specifically how this conception informs their pedagogical position.

Smith (1980) asserts that the only basic insights necessary for learning how to read are (a) print is meaningful and (b) print is different from speech. Once these two insights have been achieved and children are exposed to a variety of interesting and complex material, then reading acquisition should, Smith believes, proceed as naturally as oral language acquisition. As he states:

> I have argued that children need two basic insights to begin to learn to read. Also, I have implied that with these insights children can solve all the other problems associated with print by themselves provided that no extraneous confusion or hindrance is put in their way. They must be able to predict and make sense of language in the first place, and they can do this only by bringing meaning to it. This is certainly the way that all children learn spoken language and is probably the reason that many of them succeed in learning to read despite the instructional method used. (p. 423)

Smith's notions seem plausible, but they are totally rejected by prophets of the "phonics first" approach. Chief among these individuals is Rudolf Flesch, author of *Why Johnny Can't Read* (1955) and *Why Johnny Still Can't Read* (1981). He advances an argument long on acerbic rhetoric but decidedly short on substance.

My first objection to Flesch's conception is that he misrepresents the position of the psycholinguists, namely Smith and Goodman. He says that psycholinguistics is only look-and-say in shiny new garments (1981, pp. 23–24). But look-and-say, in the sense of focusing on one word at a time, giving word lists to memorize, and restricting vocabulary development, is definitely *not* what psycholinguistics is about at all. So any attack on those methods, and they certainly are restrictive, cannot simultaneously be a criticism of say, Smith, who seems to be Flesch's favorite target.

Aside from this, Flesch's perception of reading failure is much too simplistic. He analyzes the phenomenon without any regard to the surrounding social or social-psychological circumstances. His argument, simply put, is that reading failure is rampant because of look-and-say instruction and would be eliminated if everyone were taught by the "phonics first" method. The fallacy here, of course, is to think that any instructional method alone can guarantee students success, for any such method is but an abstraction in and of itself. Its worth can be ascertained only in a social arena of real teachers and real students. (Note that Smith's primary concern is with the nature of reading, not the teaching of reading.)

Flesch persists in his distortion by presenting the following picture of reading acquisition. Before one learns to read, the argument goes, one must know the "mechanics" of reading. In the case of phonics, one must first learn all the rules for spelling-to-sound correspondences (roughly 180 of them). Once one knows the rules one can sound out, and therefore read, any print. Typically, then, after one or two years of instruction a child can read 24,000 words, whereas a child taught another way can only read 1,000 or so words.

Again, Flesch is a proponent of sophism. If one defines reading as making sense of print, then the mere sounding out of words does not assure that such activity is taking place. But perhaps even more basic is the question of whether one can actually sound out words accurately on the basis of phonics alone. Smith submits that one cannot because the spelling-to-sound correspondences in English are not one to one, but many to many. In fact, Smith asserts, the chances of successfully sounding out a word phonetically is only one in four (1979, p. 55). He illustrates the problem.

> Here are eleven common words in each of which the initial *ho* has a different pronunciation — *hot, hope, hook, hoot, house, hoist, horse, horizon, honey, hour, honest.* Can anyone really believe that a child could learn to identify any of these words by sounding out the letters? (1979, p. 56)

He goes on to add that "phonics works if you know what a word is likely to be in the first place. . . . It is not surprising that children who are best at phonics are the best readers — they have to be" (1979, pp. 56–57).

Smith overstates his case somewhat by arguing that a program based on phonics would be too complex for even a computer to read. Flesch has countered by citing that a Kurzweil Reading Machine can, in fact, "read" by using a phonics-based program fed into a computer. But I fail to see the relevance of this information. For, alas, children are not Kurzweils, and the machine is doing what machines are made for: to do work that humans cannot do efficiently. Reading by phonics is some of that work.

The last problematic claim by Flesch is that other children will be severely limited in the number of words they can read as opposed to phonics-first readers. He has reached this conclusion by inspecting the word lists of non-phonics reading books. But I know of no evidence to show that children read only the words in their readers. Counting word lists, therefore, is by no means an accurate measure of how many words children know. If children have it set in mind to read and are actually reading in some instances, they will not allow themselves to be restricted to any reading book. Nor, I hope, will they be constrained by any teacher. Any method that tries to force them to focus on only one aspect of the reading process is harmful.

All this is not to say that phonics is irrelevant. It is one strategy for figuring out text and, as a child assembles a repertoire of strategies, there is some place for it. The essential point, however, is that a child is searching for sense and at no point should that search be hindered by dogmatic instruction. Just as one learns spoken language by total immersion in it, so it must be with reading. And so it was, I am sure, for me. Bissex (1980) has made a similar discovery. Reporting on her assiduous observation of her son she writes:

> Development—and Paul's development in particular—is not evenly paced. There is more rapid movement through the earlier strategies and concepts because these are more limited and incomplete in relation to the demands of the tasks. Especially at the beginning, quite drastic change seems essential for progress. It may not matter so much where a child begins in reading (phonics, sight words, language experience) as that he begins *somewhere* that works for him and soon moves somewhere *else*. Later strategies, being more inclusive and complex, allow room for more extended development. (p. 168)

Bissex, as is proper, sees a child's active intellect in control of the reading acquisition process. It is a blessing that children have such intellects, as well as the strength to persevere in the face of all the not-so-great debates around them.

OF LITERATURE

> Sentimental things are said about the magical world of literature and the imagination, but few think of applying this driving force to the basic learning of literacy tasks. Nor do they think of remedying the situation for those children who have not learned to operate imaginatively. For such children, half their motivation for becoming literate is paralyzed, and so learning to read must be like learning to walk with one leg. (Holdaway 1979, pp. 55–56)

Don Holdaway understands that the story, the poem, address and in turn spur our curiosity in ways more powerful than our own immediate experience. The world of fantasy opens to us whole new vistas. This is particularly true of small children, always our most eager seekers. The lure of the story is what kept me and my kindergarten class transfixed when we should have been on our way home. In listening to *Curious George* we all wanted to know what this monkey could encounter in the way of adventure, of ups and downs. Most important, we wanted to find out what we could make of his ups and downs, for by then we, of course, were having a few ups and downs ourselves. It is in such a way that literature can enlighten young lives, in fact, all lives. As Rouse (1978) tells us, "life will never be a substitute for literature, it's not long enough" (p. 92).

When listening to a story and thus expanding the limits of their conception, children receive valuable assistance in their own quests to apprehend print. Britton (1972) develops this idea:

The children who listen are gaining experience of written forms of the English language, and this aspect of the process is of particular importance to those who cannot yet read for themselves. There is an art of listening to reading that is very different from the process of listening to somebody talking to you — and this art contributes to the art of reading. (p. 150)

The young listener even before attending school can put together, in Holdaway's terms, a literacy set (p. 62). On an emotional level this involves having a high expectation of print, of viewing it as a source of pleasure and fulfillment. Linguistically the child is picking up on the types of intonation patterns, idioms, and vocabulary that are found more in print than in speech. On an operational level, the child has become aware of such predictive operations as using the context to fill in particular language slots and can also follow plot and other logical arrangements. Concerning the conventions of print itself, the child may know that it is composed from left to right, from top to bottom, left page before right page. The child may also know some letters, some phonetic principles, and may have some concept of "words" and "spaces."

Looking back at "First Lessons," we see every indication that the development of a literacy set as described above was well underway. I mentioned earlier that I was reading before formal school instruction. By doing so I probably saved myself, in a sense, from such instruction. With respect to reading I had a little edge on the school, a leg up if you will. You might even say that up there on 146th Street I had a "head start."

OF FAMILY

Denny Taylor (1983), in describing her approach to ethnographic literacy research, reports: "my task was to develop systematic ways of looking at reading and writing as activities that have consequences and are affected by family life" (p. xiii). The implication is that much literacy acquisition (like mine) goes on in the home for which the home is not given proper credit. That oversight will not be a problem here.

If I ever had a true reading teacher, it was my older sister. If anyone were explicitly manipulating my attempts to comprehend print, it was mainly she. Or perhaps I was manipulating her (probably both). For as determined as she was to show off what she knew, I was just as determined to make her display it. She was not going to leave me behind, participate on a broader level than I, share anything, especially with our mother, that I could not share. So apart from any incentive a school might provide, reading took on great significance within the confines of our very own family. It was a way not only of widening and deepening perspectives through a self-regulated encounter with story; it was a way of enhancing social status. This use of reading as a tool of social growth is seen by Taylor to be essential:

> The question emerges of whether we can seriously expect children who have never experienced or have limited experience of reading and writing as complex cultural activities to successfully learn to read and write from the narrowly defined pedagogical practices of our schools. Can we teach children on an individual level of intrapersonal processes what they have never experienced on a social level as interpersonal processes of functional utility in their everyday lives? I would submit that we cannot. (pp. 90–91)

It is clear that my early reading skills, like my oral ones, developed largely within a family context. Familial relations dictated that these skills were to be regarded as cherished possessions. My younger sister at three, poised with blade in hand, obviously understood a great deal about the social value of reading.

Impression Management

On one level this entire chapter has been about linguistic role-playing, the use of certain conventions of language to sustain various relationships. I have discussed my doing what we all do: using language as a way of adapting to situations and, to some extent, as a means of defining and controlling situations. We all practice, in Goffman's (1959) terms, the art of impression management. It is important to realize, however, that such a display of verbal ability as described above grows directly out of and then evolves alongside a general social competence. Or as Byers and Byers (1972) indicate:

> And when we examine a human relationship such as a simple conversation between two people, we almost immediately discover that there are multiple modalities or channels operating in addition to language. We discover that the modalities, verbal and nonverbal, are learned as patterns of the culture (as language is learned) and that they are systematic (as language has grammar, for example). Furthermore we discover that they all fit together: they are systematically interrelated. (p. 6)

What we see, therefore, is that there is a nonverbal grammar (or grammars) to be acquired. More will be made of this later on. But even with respect to the character we have been considering thus far, the conception is certainly convenient, and it should not be surprising that I have made quite specific remarks in the narrative about this particular set of skills.

At the close of "First Lessons," I assert that I "could play the middle or skirt the fringe as I saw fit." It was easier written than done, of course, but it is evident that I had some idea of how much an actor I had to be and had confidence that I could handle the part. I had a clear (we might even say conscious) notion of how important even nonverbal adaptation or impression management was in protecting my own developing identity. If I had landed in Rome, I certainly would have been about the business of doing as the Romans were doing—if I had thought it would help matters. I later took this heightened awareness into a dominant White environment and, because I was afforded a certain measure of participation, I picked up certain elements of the grammar of White, middle-class, particularly Jewish, nonverbal communication (such as when to make eye contact and when not to), which I in turn used to guide the impressions the residents of that environment formed (while they were of course trying to figure out and outmaneuver me). It may be an open question as to who acted better, but I undoubtedly did all right.

"All the world," Goffman writes, "is not, of course, a stage, but the crucial ways in which it isn't are not easy to specify" (p. 72). He does, nevertheless, proceed to detail the most significant difference. "An action staged in a theater is a relatively contrived illusion and an admitted one: unlike ordinary life, nothing real or actual can happen to the performed characters" (p. 254). Art may imitate life, then, but it is not nearly as difficult. The curtain was always up for me, as for most, and I was a young lad as busy as the next child learning lines, mastering gestures, working on all levels to manage impression.

While I am being so direct about impression management let me offer, in closing out this chapter, a few more phrases in trying to shape yours. The home in Harlem from which I was catapulted into the larger world was one that was, in a sociolinguistic sense, enabling—not disabling. Tensions existed that obviously helped to shape my personality in ways I have yet to fully understand, but such tensions alone did not, in fact could not, impede the acquisition of the sociolinguistic ability that has been examined in this chapter. There was a *consistency* in that habitat and, I submit, it is the apprehension of consistency that is the cognitive key to communicative development. The prime affective requirement, of course, is that the use of such skills helps to establish some social relation that is gratifying. My home, no matter what else it was, took care of me on both counts.

4
Semivoices

We came to Corona when the garbage trucks still ran three or four times a week. But it wouldn't continue that way for long. The White evacuation, of mostly Irish and Italians, was nearly complete and all community services would eventually tail off leaving Blacks and blight hand in hand, wondering if they caused each other. Folks who stayed in Harlem, Brooklyn, or the Bronx would say we had moved out to Long Island. With a twenty-minute cab ride they thought we had reached outer suburbia. It wasn't nearly so great of course, but I could see how it seemed like a decent deal to families fleeing from tenements. Back then you could purchase a respectable two-family house for ten to fifteen thousand dollars, probably under the GI bill, rent out the top floor, and maybe see a comparatively rosy future. In our case we even got new furniture on credit. And we were on one of the nicest blocks in the neighborhood, tree-lined 34th Avenue, a block and a half east of Junction Boulevard. That was a street most aptly named for it served as a border between two neighborhoods, Corona and Jackson Heights, and between two worlds — a Black one and a White one. Junction Boulevard was often referred to as the Mason-Dixon line in Queens.

I was fairly pleased. The basement and backyard held good possibilities for hideaway and play, and there was a park right in the next block with seesaws, swings, the works. No Eighth Avenue. But not all that bad.

We were located virtually equidistant between P.S. 92 on 99th Street in Corona and P.S. 149 on 94th Street in Jackson Heights. They were both located on 34th Avenue and Sherry and I could spot them from in front of the house. We had no idea which way to go until our mother came outside with the baby carriage and headed east toward the dark-complexioned 92. I kept right on her heels, excited. We were turned away from that school, something about overcrowding and new zoning, and directed to 149. I kept on her heels, still excited, across the Mason-Dixon.

After Sherry and I were registered, the principal, Mr. Price escorted us to class. His pants were too baggy and long. The back of the cuffs flapped up under his heels as he walked. We thought it was funny that he should want to ruin his pants that way, and all the way down the hall we fought the urge to burst out laughing. I didn't feel very humored, though, when he ushered me into Class 1-1 and exposed me to a room full of White kids. I trembled. I wanted to grab hold of one of Mr. Price's baggy trouser legs like it was a mother's apron, but I couldn't allow myself to show that much fear. I wished Sherry would come in but when I realized she wouldn't I wished the same shock on her wherever she went. Or worse. It's like they were trying to stare me back out of the room. Goldstein. Rubin. Landau. Weiss. Cohen. I knew next to nothing about kids like that. Only saw them on the subway a couple of times and in the doctor's office downtown. My eyes frantically searched theirs, trying to find some sign I could translate into friendliness. There was one Black student, a girl in pigtails, and she stared as hard as anyone else. Mr. Price spoke at last.

"Hello class, this is Raymond Keith Gilyard." The name suddenly sounded important to me. "He's a fine enough young man, isn't he?" They answered in synchronized yesses. The principal continued. "What shall we call you, young Master Gilyard? Shall we call you Raymond or Keith?"

Nobody had ever called me Raymond before. Uptown it was always Keith or Keithy or Little Gil. Raymond was like a fifth wheel. A spare. And that's what I decided to make these people call me. *They cannot meet Keith now. I will put someone else together for them and he will be their classmate until further notice. That will be the first step in this particular survival plan.* Of course it wasn't thought out in those specific terms, but the instinct and action were there. And from that day on, through all my years in public school, all White folks had to call me Raymond.

The point was to have a plot. To keep a part of myself I could trust. A way to pull myself through. Be a Raymond, a brother, a son, a Keith, a son, a Raymond, a son, a brother. Keep juggling and save myself. So along with handwriting drills, simple addition, simple subtraction, and readings from the primer, I began getting familiar with these strange people around me. Peeping into their lives while trying to keep their strange pale noses out of mine.

One day Sherry and I were nearing Junction Boulevard while walking home when I noticed that the moon was up already. The sun, of course, was shining brightly. I was startled because I had always thought that their relationship was strictly causal. The moon came up because the sun went down or the sun went down because the moon had to come up, you know, I had that kind of notion. This was weird.

"Hey Sherry, you see that?"

"See what?"

"See the moon, Sherry. See it's up already."

"Oh yeah, I see it."

"But the sun is still up. I don't see how they can be up at the same time." She looked back over her shoulder to check. Remained silent as I continued. "You ever seen it like this before, Sherry? You ever seen this?"

"No" she finally replied. "I don't look at the sky all that much in the daytime. That's dumb. I like the stars at night. It's just like this today anyway, that's all. Just today."

"Wonder if Ma knows about this."

"You know she does. She knows about stuff like this."

"You'll ask her?"

"You can ask her, Keith."

"No, you. It'll be better. She won't get mad."

"Oh Keith, she won't get mad if you ask her something like this."

"I don't know. She might . . . you know it too!" She reflected a moment, knowing I was right.

Moms patiently explained to Sherry that her observation wasn't anything all that unusual, just the natural movement of heavenly bodies. She told her that if she would watch the sky more often, she would see it occur more often, and if she lived long enough she would see far more stranger things than that.

Indeed I have. But imagine again how I felt. The sun and the moon out together.

Sky-watching became more serious in the second grade. The Space Bug had bitten America, artificial satellites and such, and the schools had caught a fever. We were given a frenzied assortment of data about Venus, Mars, red and yellow stars, Big and Little Dippers, and Halley's comet. Seemed like I could spend all evening gazing at the stars and yakking about the universe. And I heard people say I was as bright as a star myself. I guess they meant I was motivated. I had to be to keep up with the smarter pupils in my class. And I definitely meant to keep up. To fit in.

I was the only Black in the one-level class because Saundra Meritt, whom I had grown to like during our time together in first grade, was placed in 2-3. Nowadays in public schools they may designate classes by room numbers like 2-301 or 2-315. There may be differences in performance levels among the classes but the students, at least the younger ones, may not be acutely aware of them. Probably better that way. But back in '59 I knew I was in with the so-called cream of my grade level. Even without the class numbers, the few dark faces I saw in each of the other classes made it easy to figure out what was going on. I had been "identified." I was, however, gaining more and more confidence in my role as student.

Along with Eddie Goldstein I became a class clown. We came up with the funniest quips and made the funniest faces. But we both wanted to be laughed with, not laughed at, so we scored highly on all our tests and raised our hands as vigorously as anyone else. I liked being able to play it either way. I also began expressing a certain physical dominance in the schoolyard, as I could outwrestle any of my classmates. This was as much due to aggression as to my skill. I could handle these people. And Mrs. Lehrman didn't hassle me much. She occasionally had to put my clowning in check, but her main beef seemed to be the way I would dot an *i*. I still hear her sometimes: They're just dots, Raymond. Not giant colored-in circles. Dots. Dots. Dots. Not anything so terribly important. If that was her major complaint against me I knew I had to be progressing satisfactorily. I even had an opportunity to show off for my father.

He showed up on one of those parents' observation days in a brown suit with a gray Ban-Lon shirt and a tan raincoat. When he came through the door all heads turned toward me. Then Linda Katz, as if she alone knew the scoop, tapped me on the shoulder from behind and whispered the obvious: "There goes your father, Raymond." Pops didn't bother to look my way, simply nodded to the teacher and strode swiftly to the back of the room where several other parents were already gathered.

We were working with the calendar. It was the fourteenth and Mrs. Lehrman wanted to know who could show her which date was exactly one week away. Hands shot up all around the room. Nearly everyone wanted to pounce on such an easy question, and I was among the most desperate. Waving my hand wildly and straining forward half out of my seat, squirming like I had to go to the bathroom or something, moaning, "Ooh ooh ooh Mrs. Lehrman, ooh!" She studied the contorted pleas on our faces, in our eyes. She hesitated as if she were trying to select a proper head of lettuce and then settled on Helen Rubin, who hadn't even raised her hand. Her mother was in the back, yet the girl still wasn't eager. It didn't seem fair she should be called on before I was.

I tried to attract my father's attention to let him know I knew the answer, but he was staring straight ahead. It was ironic because I had learned what I knew about the calendar from watching him run his finger down the left margin of the one in our kitchen in order to count the Sundays. There just couldn't have been any easier question for me.

But Helen had it. She accepted the rubber-tipped pointer from the teacher and stuck it straight in the box marked 20. I couldn't believe she blew it like that. Hands shot up all over again, even more urgently, and Helen was told to sit down. I didn't bother raising my hand this time because I had become more interested in Helen's mother. She was wringing her hands. She lowered her head, then lifted it slowly and blew a thin stream of air from her mouth. I imagined her in a cartoon with steam spouting from her ears, forming a scowling mist over her graying head. I was still having fun with this vision as Bernie Cohen went up and pointed to 15. Eddie called him stupid and Bernie's father was in the back smiling. Fake. I could feel it. I turned my eyes back to Mrs. Rubin's anger.

"RAYMOND." I whirled to face the teacher. I was nervous because I thought she was going to reprimand me for not paying attention and it was certainly no time for that, but when she asked "Can you show us?" it took all the control I could muster to refrain from howling with laughter.

"I think I can show you, Mrs. Lehrman."

"Well let's hop to it then." She looked back at the group of observers and asked rhetorically, "We are having our little adventures today, aren't we?"

I fidgeted with my notebook, opened and shut my inkwell a few times, you know, appearing uncertain so I could build the suspense. I slowly rose to my feet, very deliberately tucked in my shirt, and hitched my trousers. Show time. I took the pointer from Mrs. Lehrman, switched it from hand to hand, tapped the floor with the rubber tip a couple of times, and picked out that glorious 21.

"Thank you Raymond" said Mrs. Lehrman in relief. She smiled and I poked out my chest and headed for my seat. Cast a glance at Pops. He wasn't one for the big grin, but his faint nod of approval let me know he was pleased.

It would have been better still if Pops could have caught my act a few weeks later when Mrs. Lehrman asked if anyone knew the difference between a house and a home. No one else in the class even attempted an answer. The perfect stage for me. I mean getting called on and supplying the correct response was exciting enough, but you knew there were other young knights who could have handled the question. To dominate the floor completely, however, was to be top royalty. And there I was, the king.

"A house can be anywhere you live with walls and ceilings and floors. But it's not a home until there is love." This answer seemed to really excite the teacher.

"That is well put, Raymond. Very, very interesting." I sat down as my classmates stared in amazement, probably wondering where I picked up this information. I wouldn't tell them I had learned it in Sunday School. And I was really somewhat amazed myself that not a single one of them could answer that question. I began to wonder more seriously about what these Jews were learning in those synagogues and those one-afternoon-a-week Hebrew School classes. What were the few Catholics, who got out early on Wednesdays for religious instruction, learning over at Blessed Sacrament?

I felt I was coming along nicely. Sang "America the Beautiful" and "My Country, 'Tis of Thee" as loudly as anyone. Recited the pledge of allegiance at a time when it was mandatory to do so. Related strongly to "Jack and the Beanstalk" and felt great admiration for both Androcles and the lion. Thought Miles Standish was a hero for fighting Indians and beheading Wituwamat. Respected wig-wearing, silver dollar-slinging George Washington, Honest Abe, and President Eisenhower. Showed the proper concern for the Cold War, was glad Red China was denied entry to the U.N., and was properly upset when a spying Francis Gary Powers was shot down from the Russian skies. Smooth sailing on into 3-1. Where I punched Susan Goldberg straight in her eye.

The boys, mainly John Greenberg and Michael Stein, conned me into it. They had some kind of running feud with the girls and wanted to end it, so they drew up this peace treaty that they wanted the girls to approve. The whole thing was silly to me because I never categorically hated girls. I also knew that over at P.S. 92 that type of thing couldn't be happening because for those boys, like myself, there wasn't a hate-girls phase to emerge from. Hell, some guys over there were hard pursuing the girls right from jumpstreet. Trying to corner them on the back stairs or in the wardrobe closet. A boy-girl feud, in and of itself, didn't appeal to me at all. Nor did resolving one. White girls' acceptance wasn't what I needed anyway. I would long for a certain measure of it later on at classroom parties when, although I knew I could dance rings around everyone else, I had to pretend to dislike dancing. I knew no girl could really be comfortable with me as a partner. So I left them alone. But I had to be tight with the boys, so when John told me during lunch hour that I could be their general if I could get Susan, the leader of the girls, to sign the treaty, I agreed to give it a try. Couldn't turn down a generalship, not even a peace time one, and I kept sending Susan notes all that afternoon to persuade her to sign. She ripped up all the notes and stuffed the pieces into her desk. I sent her the treaty itself and she ripped that also. I had to send Michael a message to write another one. When I approached Susan after school she was in the middle of a group of girls heading farther into Jackson Heights. I blocked her path and offered the replacement treaty.

"Look Susan, you don't really have to sign it but at least you could read it. You might change your mind." Without uttering a word, she stepped around me, leaving me to present my case to thin air if I so desired. The boys around me began giggling. Even John flashed his braces. I ran in front of her again and shoved the paper at her. "READ IT I SAID." She merely started around me again. I grabbed her by the shoulder while warning her, "You're not gonna just ignore me." She shook loose from my grasp, seemingly unafraid, chumping me off some more.

"I'm not reading that. It's so stupid."

"Oh yeah? Well you're still gonna read it. And you're gonna sign it too."

"I'm not signing anything."

"Yeah? Then I think I'll sign you." I uncorked a beauty of a right hand straight to her left eye. She went one way and her book bag went the other.

"You bastard" she screamed as she covered her eye momentarily with her hands. "You're a real bastard." I wanted to slug her again but my fear was swelling even faster than her eye was.

"You all right Susan?" I asked stupidly.

"Leave me alone you bastard! Leave me alone!" She picked up her bag and started running for home. I took off in the opposite direction, knowing I was in deep trouble, and figuring I had until morning to figure a way to escape it. Good thing neither Sherry nor Judy knew what had happened, so I could at least avoid the beating that night. After the next morning though, I would definitely be fair game if I failed to come up with a plan.

That next morning Susan was not in class. Nobody who was there offered me any conversation. The girls were mad I suppose, or scared. The boys were waiting to take their cue from me. Mrs. Rosen didn't seem to know what was going on. I remained silently worried, could see no way to get around what I imagined would be the most ferocious beating of my life. To get in trouble at home was bad enough, but to act up in public was the worst thing I could do to Moms. Wherever we traveled folks always commented on how well behaved my sisters and I were. Moms would usually reply, "They had better be." And that was the truth.

It was about an hour before I was summoned to the principal's office. Susan had a terrible shiner and turned her head to avoid my stare. Mr. Price sternly directed me to a seat facing her. Susan's parents had come and gone. Guess they had confidence in Mr. Price. I was glad I didn't have to face them.

"I won't beat around the bush, Raymond" said Mr. Price as he sank into his chair. "Is this what you are taught at home?"

"No Mr. Price" I replied humbly, glancing at the floor. "I just lost my temper and I feel sorry about it. I want Susan to know I'm sorry too." She still wouldn't look me in the eye. Mr. Price continued.

"An apology is nice, Raymond. But it won't help her eye feel any better. I'll have to inform your parents. You understand that, don't you?"

"Yes Mr. Price." I felt I was officially finished. What shall I tell them?"

"I don't know." I spoke in a forlorn semiwhisper, you know, doomed but looking for a miracle of sympathy. Then I looked Mr. Price fairly straight in the eye. "Probably have to tell them I was being real bad and punched a girl in the eye for nothing."

"For no reason at all?"

"No Mr Price. I had a reason but it wasn't a good one."

"What reason is that, Raymond?"

"I was mad because she wouldn't listen to me."

"Oh I see. You mean she wouldn't acknowledge that whole peace treaty affair?"

"She wouldn't even read it."

"It's a free country" Susan cut in. "I don't have to do anything I don't want to do."

"But you could have listened" I retorted. I could feel my anger rising. BUT HAD TO CHECK IT. Susan countered sharply.

"I didn't want to. It was so stupid . . . and they made you do it."

"They did not" I blurted. "I did it myself."

"You're stupid then."

"I am not." I was ready to shine her other eye but I quickly put the emotion in harness. Had to appear remorseful. Mr. Price cut in.

"Now, now. No one is stupid here. What we have here is an example of what bad judgment and a lack of discipline can lead to. Do you know what discipline means, Raymond?"

"Yes Mr. Price. It's like self-control."

"Precisely. You know I can tell you a great deal about discipline because of my experiences in the Navy. Was your father ever in the service?"

"He was in the Navy too" I said proudly. Actually he had been in the Army but you know how I had to play it.

"Then I'm sure he can back me up. You see, I had to learn how to follow rules in the Navy. I had my own emotions; there were many things I did not like; I felt misunderstood a lot of the time, but I still had to follow the rules. Nothing was more important than the rules. If we didn't have rules, we couldn't have gotten anything accomplished. There would have been no cooperation, and without cooperation there would not have been any Navy. And that just wouldn't have been right. Can you understand that?"

"Yes." Sure I could. I knew there were few things in life worse than not having a navy.

"Now we can't have a school without cooperation either, without rules. And our rules state that we do not hit each other. Is that clear?"

"Yes Mr. Price." I struggled to gaze at him directly so he could read how sincere I was. "I know we're not supposed to fight."

"Of course not Raymond. And we certainly can't beat up the girls. Gentlemen don't do that. You do want to be a gentleman, don't you?"

"Yes Mr Price. I want to be a gentleman."

"That's good." He paused briefly, seemed pleased that I was so agreeable. "So tell me, is there any chance this might happen again?"

"Not with me. I'll never do anything like this again."

"Are you sure?"

"Yes Mr. Price. I'd never do this again because I know it's bad." I had locked in on his eyes real good for a moment.

"I hope you're right. You know kids get thrown out of school for things like this. Would your parents wish that to happen to you?"

"No sir. My parents wouldn't like that at all."

"I think not." A fleeting smile passed over his face as he looked over at Susan, who was already focused in on him. "What do you think, Susan? Can you trust him? Has he ever done anything like this before?"

"No. This is the first time he ever bothered anybody."

"So maybe you can trust him now?"

"I don't know. He might try something else."

"Well I can't let him do that. I'd have to kick him out of here before I let him do that. As a matter of fact, if you don't think you can feel comfortable around him, I can still move him. Do you think I should do that?"

Susan pointed her shiner directly at me and I lowered my head. Might be kissing 149 goodbye. She spoke very deliberately.

"Let him stay. . . . He likes this school."

"And you'll feel safe? I want you to be sure."

"I'll be all right, Mr. Price."

"O.K." he said smilingly. "We'll see how it goes."

The principal rose to escort Susan from the office. I rubbed my face with my hands. I had been played out of position by the boys and I knew it. As angry as I was I thought they might need a peace treaty to ever talk to me again. I was sure wishing I could get Moms to sign one. After a few moments Mr. Price returned, patted me on the head, then resumed his seat.

"So you really feel sorry, don't you?" I locked in on his eyes again.

"Yes I do."

"I know you do. I believe that. Tell me, do you like it here?"

"I like it here a whole lot." Anybody in my world could have answered that one for him.

"Do you have friends in class?"

"Oh yeah. I have a lot of friends in the class. I like everybody."

He leaned back in his chair and looked upward, staring so intently at the ceiling that I looked up also. But wasn't anything up there I could see that was going to help me. Finally Mr. Price continued.

"I'm going to offer you a deal, Master Gilyard. If you promise to behave yourself, to practice more discipline from now on, I won't tell your parents about what happened yesterday. Do you think we can make an arrangement of that sort?"

Now you just know we could. I mean I was getting the biggest break since Noah was allowed to beat the flood. I floated all the way back to class, eager to maintain my end of the bargain. Which I did pretty well. I was still admonished here and there about chattering and clowning, but I never dared do anything serious enough to get Mr. Price involved again. Susan and I were forced together. Every time there was a group project, like reporting on the Northeastern states or something, Mrs. Rosen made sure to put us in the same group. I even had to go to her home for a couple of meetings, and she became my favorite girl in the class.

I was a hero with the boys and John said I could still be their general since I had the most courage. I flatly refused that commission. Didn't want to be a colonel either. Or a major. We finally decided that captain would be a good rank for me, you know, in the middle.

The boys and girls started working things out for themselves. As for myself, I was on course even steadier than ever. Spelling tests. Book reports. Multiplication. Division. History. Astronomy. Current events. Mr. Price came on the loudspeaker to request we give a moment of silence for U.N. Secretary-General Hammarskjold, who died in a plane crash while on the way to take care of some business in the Congo. Kennedy was in, took our class decisively, and we were in the era of manned space flights. We jammed the auditorium to listen to the radio broadcast of Alan B. Shepard's joy ride aboard the Freedom 7. I clapped in tune with everyone else. Yes sir, Raymond was doing fine.

Keith was developing well also. Found my first best friend, Lonnie Blair, while I was walking down 97th Street on the way to the store. He

was in front of his house throwing pebbles up onto his own roof. He held
the bunch in his left hand and plucked and tossed them with his right.
He was a skinny, close-cropped young boy, very much like myself. When
he noticed me approaching, he dropped the pebbles right where he stood
and came up straight to my face.

"Hey boy, what's your name?"

"My name Keith."

"Oh yeah?"

"Yeah. What's your name?"

"Ain't none a your damn business. That's what the hell it is."

"Well mine ain't none a yours then."

"Is too 'cause you just told me your name stupid."

"I did not."

"Did so."

"What I say?"

"Said your name was Keith, dummy. Can't remember what you just
said?"

"I was just foolin you."

"You wasn't foolin me, Keith. You can't."

He did have me on that one and I didn't like it one bit. I stepped
around him and continued on my way. He kept following, paused to pick
up a rock and hurl it up on a neighbor's roof, then pulled alongside.

"You know I seen you before in school."

"So I seen you too."

"Yeah Keith, but I seen you first 'cause I always see people first before
they see me. Where you use to live at?"

"I come from Harlem."

"Harlem? I heard about that place. That means you 'pose to be tough
or somethin? You ain't as tough as people from Brooklyn."

"That's where you from?"

"Yeah Keith, that's where I'm from!"

"So that don't make you so tough."

"Tougher than you."

"No you not."

"Yes I am Keith. What if I did somethin to you? What would you do?"

"Do somethin back to you."

"Like what?"

"You'll see. I'm use ta fightin. I been in gang fights."

"Aw man, get outa here. You ain been in no gang fights."

"I have so. Where you think I got this scar from?" I put a hand up
to the left side of my face to really draw his attention to it. I closed in

on him, but kept enough distance so that out of the corner of my eye I could watch his reaction. He really appreciated that scar. I had an edge on him, had him leaning toward belief.

"How that happen?"

"I told you I was in a gang fight. I got cut with a butcher knife. You don't know about stuff like that. You too little."

"I'm just as big as you" he said defiantly.

"Yeah but you couldn't get out like I could. When everybody in my house was sleepin I use to sneak out at midnight. That's when the big people had the gang fights. I was the only kid they let in. This big man cut me and I was bleeding a lot but my side got him."

"Did they kill him?" he asked eagerly.

"Yeah they killed him. What you think?"

"Well they 'pose to anyway. I was in gang fights too you know."

"Where's your scar then?"

"You don't have to have one."

"Yes you do. If you was in one you have to have a scar. If you was in a *real* one."

I knew I scored heavily with that tale, so did he, and we had set up a pretty good basis for a friendship. Neither one of us was going to be bullied.

On days when I would break off early from my classmates so I could catch up to the Black group heading toward Corona, I would always fall in stride next to Lonnie as we waited to see where the next fun would come from. We both had a lot of static, but for different reasons. Lonnie plain liked to rumble. Enjoyed it about as much as anything. I preferred to spar with words. Debate, you know, try to rank somebody out. I usually had to fight only when someone lost his temper because I was needling too good, getting too good an audience response. Of course I'd also fight if my target tried to ignore me. And sometimes I had to use my best rap to cop pleas to older kids who got a little too aggressive from time to time. I usually was able to be just humble enough to suit them and just assertive enough to save face within my own inner circle.

Lonnie and I often roamed Junction Park together. One day, when we were both nine, we were on the seesaw. Suddenly, while I was on the up end of the board, he jumped off, leaving me to crash painfully to the ground. I was jarred from head to toe. As soon as I shook off most the pain I charged straight at Lonnie and we locked in one of our special tussles. We had our own ground rules; we only wrestled, never kicked or punched each other as we would an outsider. After a couple of rolls along the ground I managed to get him in a headlock. He yelled "I give" even before I could secure my hold and apply any serious pressure. Neither of us had ever given up that easily. I let him go but was prepared for some kind of trick. However, he just walked over to the nearest bench, sat down, and started laughing. I was still waiting for the trick when he spoke.

"You know somethin Keith? We should become blood brothers."

"Blood brothers? What's that?"

"What's that?" he mimicked. "You mean you don't even know what it is?"

"Yeah I know. I mean I used to know but I forgot. What we have to do?"

"It's easy. All we do is stick needles in our fingers and rub our blood together. That makes us like real brothers and we always help each other out with things."

"But we do that now."

"Yeah but this is a real special thing. You want a brother, don't you?" You know he couldn't get any argument from me.

"When can we do it?"

"Right now" he replied as he began pulling a wad of tissues from his pocket. There was a small sewing needle inside. "You ain scared, is you?"

"Naw I ain scared. It's just like a doctor's needle, that's all. I ain scared a no doctor's needle so I ain scared a this."

"Yeah all right. Gimme your left hand then. It's the one closer to your heart."

"How you know that?"

"I just know, man. Gimme the hand." I offered it promptly this time and Lonnie deftly pricked a hole in the tip of my index finger, setting forth a rush of adventure. He pricked his own finger and we pressed our blood together. "Now we brothers Keith."

That was perfect. Especially since it didn't look as though the real thing was coming along. Now if he could only be in my class. I always thought Lonnie Blair was as smart as any kid I knew. He just wouldn't take much of an interest in school. Back then I would still try to turn him around. I worked straight into my pitch.

"I'm glad we're like real brothers now. We ain gon let nobody mess with us. If you was in my class that would really be good."

"3-1 class? Not me. Here, take this tissue man. Your finger still bleedin." As I accepted the tissue Lonnie kept emphasizing his rejection of my idea. "Fuck the 3-1 class. Yall startin ta git too much homework. Shoot, that's what's takin you so long to git back outside now. Makin sure all them arithmetic problems git done right. We don't worry about all that in 3-4. I hardly ever do my homework and I still don't git in that much trouble. Shoot, you don't do yours one day and you might git a note home with your sister. Nah, I wouldn't want no one class. Don't want *no* class." Lonnie seemed to dive off into deep thought for a moment. Then he switched topics altogether. "Hey man, let's git back on the seesaw."

Sure. And it has been that way a lot of the time for me and Lonnie, my brother, my first best friend. On different planes of reality despite our closeness. Years and years on the seesaw. But whenever our feet hit the ground at the same time. Beautiful.

Home provided still more difficulties to resolve and there were no easy resolutions. I had lumps to take there also. Especially during the 1960 World Series. Along with the rest of the boys in my class who cared about baseball, I had become an incurable New York Yankees fan even though I knew my mother would never approve. She was from the Ebbets Field Asylum, you know, if it wasn't Don Newcombe and Gil Hodges then it wasn't really baseball. The Dodgers had already left town, but she was still loyal. She would pull for them and every other team in the National League to smash the hated Yankees. That is, every team except the San Francisco Giants. Pops, you see, was a Giants fan. And although he was far less zealous about his loyalty than my mother was, there was no way I could drum up any support in our household for the local heroes. Moms said the Yankees were a prejudiced team, reluctant to sign Negroes. Well by then they had Elston Howard and Hector Lopez and that seemed to me to be Negro enough for a baseball team. I didn't know yet what the Jackie Robinson experiment had been all about. I simply wanted the Yankees to crush the upstart, overconfident Pittsburgh Pirates. And I was sure they would do it because they had such an awesome lineup and had been playing so well. Mantle, Maris, and company had cracked 193 homers for a new American League record, had finished the season with fifteen consecutive victories. I knew Dick Groat had hit .325 for the Pirates and was the man to keep a rally going, but I wasn't worried. We had too many home runs in our bats for their little rallies to overcome. No, no one should take the Pirates too seriously.

I panicked when the Pirates won the opener 6–4. But when Mickey Mantle knocked two over the wall the next day to key a 16–3 rout, my mental peace was restored. Now all we had to do was bring them up to the Stadium and polish them off. And when Mickey cracked another homer and Bobby Richardson weighed in with a grand slam behind the shutout pitching of Whitey Ford, I was ready for the celebration. It was inconceivable that the Yankees would drop the next two games. I was severely depressed, couldn't understand how we could score only four runs in two whole games when we often scored more than four runs in a single inning. Now we were only one loss away from losing the whole

World Series. And Moms was ribbing me real good. She was on vacation and was a most interested spectator.

"Boy, I don't know what possessed you to like those Yankees." I don't know if it occurred to her that I was simply rooting for the home team. "You see they're nothing but clowns. Getting ready to lose the Series. Pirates gonna go bop bop bop tomorrow." She spoke while taking three swings with an imaginary bat to illustrate her point. Unwisely, I threw her a fast ball straight down the middle.

"The Yankees are gonna win the next game, Ma. You watch how they beat those Priates."

"Beat them? Boy you need to stop babbling all that foolishness before folks come and lock you up. Beat the Pirates? Hmph. They couldn't beat them with a stick."

"Just watch Mickey Mantle, Ma. Just watch."

"Yeah. Watch him strike out some more."

"He doesn't always strike out. You see he has three home runs already. You know he's good."

"Yeah he's good. A good joke. Boy, you got too much faith in that Mickey Mantle, but I'll tell you something: Mickey Mantle couldn't hit the side of a barn with an ironing board. The Yankees will lose the next game, JUST LIKE THEY LOST THE LAST ONE, and then you'll see that the National League is the best."

"You just don't know, Ma."

"No you're the one who just doesn't know. I've already forgotten things you haven't even learned yet."

"Yeah I know, Ma. But what's gonna happen in the next game is the future."

"Sure it's the future. But it will be the sad, sad past for the Yankees soon enough." She laughed and went bop bop bop some more. I wasn't qualified to beat her with words. Nor could I break the hold she had on Sherry and Judy. Neither of them could tell you the difference between a curve ball and a jock strap, but they hated the Yankees. And they were working on Debra Lynn.

Whitey Ford came through with another shutout to tie the Series at 3–3 and I was ecstatic. I didn't get a chance to gloat and brag too much because my mother, predictably, wouldn't permit it. When she heard me deriding Sherry and Judy she told me to be quiet so that I wouldn't wake up Debra Lynn. But I knew neither the noise nor my little sister's sleep was the real issue. And I knew that my mother wanted that deciding seventh game just as much as I did. However, I knew she wouldn't get it. I figured Mantle and company had lost a few games to keep this thing exciting. Of course I would have preferred for them to whack out the Pirates in four straight. But if they wanted to win in seven games, for ultimate suspense, I could accept it.

The next afternoon I was daydreaming in class about how the Yankees were down in Pittsburgh knocking balls all over the field and into the stands. I had them leading 18–0 after seven innings, humiliating the entire town. I imagined I had become a grown man while my mother had become a little eight-year-old girl. I'm not sure whether she was my daughter or not. We were watching the game on television and she was frightfully upset because the Pirates were losing so badly. I patted her on the head and whispered softly, "Don't cry little Margie. It's only a game. Maybe your team can win the World Series next year." I didn't tease this little girl.

I went into shock after school when I heard on Michael Stein's transistor radio that the Pirates had just rallied for five runs off of Bobby Shantz and Jim Coates in the bottom of the eighth to go ahead 9–7 and that Tony Kubek, whom I thought invented the shortstop position, had been forced out of the game when Bill Virdon's grounder hit a stone and hit him in the throat.

"Don't worry Raymond" Michael said gravely. "We'll catch up."

I sped home to watch it happen.

Moms was already enjoying herself when I came in. "It's bop bop bop just like I told you it would be. Come on in here and see those Yankees of yours get beat." I was silent, sank limply into a chair, and prayed.

Bobby Richardson looped a single to left-center and Dale Long followed with a hit to right, sending Richardson to third base. Gil McDougald came in to run for Long. The manager yanked Bob Friend and brought in Harvey Haddix to pitch. Maris, Mantle, and Yogi Berra were coming to bat. It definitely looked like a big inning was blooming.

"All right Harvey, let's strike them out. Be hard on em sugar. Be hard." I silently opposed her. Come on Roger. Pleeezzz. My legs were shaking now and I was clutching the arms of the chair with my clammy fingers. Pleeezzzzz!

Maris popped out, runners holding the bases, and up came the magnificent Mantle.

"Here's an easy one, Harvey darling. Just throw it through the hole in his bat. Watch your big shot now, Keith. Watch him."

Mantle ripped a single to right scoring Richardson to make it 9–8 and sending McDougald around to third base and me up out of my seat. "Yeah we gon git em now. We gon git em now. Here comes Yogi."

"That don't mean nothin. He'll either strike out or hit into a double play."

"No he ain't, Ma." I couldn't be any more rebellious vocally but I figured my mother had to be off her rocker if she thought Yogi would strike out or hit into a double play. All of New York knew that there wasn't a better hitter in the clutch than old Yogi.

But Berra wasn't too spectacular this time. He smashed a drive toward first which Rocky Nelson fielded before stepping on the bag. Two outs. He whirled to try to nail Mantle at second base to end the game, but Mickey was sneaking back to first and, though their bodies collided, Mickey beat the tag. McDougald crossed the plate and the score was tied.

"Yay Mickey. I knew we could catch up."

"Aw boy, now they playin dirty. You see how he tripped that man to get back to the base? He cheatin, but it won't get him too far."

"He didn't trip him. They just fell together."

"He tripped him plain as day. Ain't you got eyes?"

Moose Skowron grounded out to end the inning but I wasn't overly worried. I was sure Ralph Terry could hold the Pirates until we could get another turn at the plate. But he failed! Mazeroski smacked the second pitch over the left field wall and the game was over. Merry fans swarmed the field as Mazeroski rounded the bases with his arm swirling, hat in hand. My throat grew lumpy and tears began rolling down my cheeks. Moms was very happily into one of her bop bop bop routines.

"Here's how he did it. He just closed his eyes and went bop."

"He did not close his eyes!" The tears were coming heavy now, and I was sniffling.

"Yes he did, boy. He closed his eyes and knocked it over the wall. What? Are you crying over this game? Don't be so silly. You shouldn't have been rooting for those stupid Yankees in the first place. Now they got you cryin. Look at Yogi. He cryin. Your great Mickey, he'll be cryin too. They'll know better next time they fool around with these Pittsburgh Pirates. And here you cryin over a little old ballgame."

The tears kept flowing. How could God twist the Series so badly? The Yankees outscored the Pirates 55–27 and still lost the Series. In the locker room afterward, Mickey stated "This is the first time that we lost a Series when I know we should have won." Yeah Mick. I know what you mean.

I was too often too sensitive around the house I suppose, but it certainly wasn't all tears. There was the pure joy of watching Debra Lynn grow and learn to make mud pies, of secretly outracing the bees to the white and gold honeysuckles in our neighbor's forbidden yard, of helping Judy master the first grade, of twisting with Sherry and Chubby Checker, of staying up to help Guy Lombardo bring in the new year, running outside with Sherry and Judy and waving west, toward Manhattan, and yelling with all our might, "Goodbye 1960. Goodbye."

It's about this time that my father comes front and center. I remember studying him very closely. Saw the annoyance on his face when I ripped yet another pair of pants at the knee. Saw the pride when I solved yet another math problem. Saw the determination in his stride as he went up the block to recover my baseball glove, which had been stolen because I hadn't kept close enough watch on it in the schoolyard. I would have fought the boy if I was sure he had the glove. But he kept denying he had it—until my father showed up. And when our family went out to Coney Island I watched Pops swim boldly out into the ocean, left us wading near the shore. He went out so far we could barely see him, out farther than anyone else. Sherry became nervous.

"He might drown all the way out there."

"Nah, he ain gon drown out there. He can swim all the way to Spain if he wants to. He can swim!"

And he could make you laugh also. He'd sit at the kitchen table and yawn loud and long like a siren. Then he might burst out singing the food song, matching meals to the days of the week. I'd get confused sometimes about which day to link up with the roast beef, but I'd be right with him by the time we hit the weekend:

Today is Friday, today is Friday
Friday's fi-ish
Is everybody happy?
Oh I should say.

Maybe not. Pops was showing up in my bed at night quite regularly. I really didn't know anything was wrong because I had a notion that it was all right for fathers to hang out that way with their little sons. Only when he moved upstairs into a room set off from the rest of the apartment up there did I recognize the separation for what it was. I didn't ask many questions about it and didn't receive much of an explanation. I still didn't know about slow horses and fast women.

My mother went to a parent-teacher conference that spring. I was glad she attended because I had a couple of compositions up on the bulletin board. When she returned home, she immediately began beating me across my back with the ironing cord. I had no time to concoct a defense. Hell, I didn't even know what the charge was. Only when she fell into her groove was the meaning of her action revealed.

"So you fightin people in school hunh?"

"No Ma, no, ooch ooch owww. . . .

"Don't lie to me boy. You know you punched that girl Susan in her eye."

"Ouch ouch . . . but . . . but ouch. . . .

It was going to be my worst beating yet. I wanted to annihilate Mrs. Rosen, who I figured had spilled the beans.

Hung around a lot with Lonnie Blair that summer. Got better at stick-ball and fighting. Watched Mantle and Maris chase Babe Ruth's home run record, and kept an eye on Frank Robinson and the Cincinnati Reds, who appeared as if they would win the National League pennant and provide the October opposition for the Yankees. And I was especially mindful of Virgil Ivan Grissom's flight aboard the Liberty Bell 7, you know, had to keep Raymond sharp for another one class.

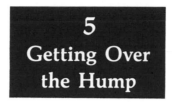

5
Getting Over the Hump

In the memoirs and/or case studies of Jonathan Kozol (1968), Gerald Levy (1970), and Daniel Fader (1971), the third grade is cited as a critical juncture in the elementary school education of African-American, urban, public school students. Each of these writers believes that these children for the most part enter public school with normal to high levels of self-esteem and a matching eagerness to learn, but typically fall behind academically by the end of the third grade, as they have found academic pursuit unfulfilling and have begun to retreat from the process. This perception has been confirmed many times in the literature (give or take a grade). The obvious conclusion to draw from such consensus is that African-American students will indeed develop the academic ability to succeed throughout public school if they can but weather the early years, can but get over the hump.

In this chapter I will assess my own school pilgrimage through that apparently crucial third grade, analyzing the factors that allowed me to negotiate the passage in fairly good academic shape. However, I must first consider why so many researchers feel that it is such a formidable task for a Black child to complete four years of public schooling — and actually enjoy doing it. Toward this end I will provide a historical sketch of the general nature of public schools and describe how Blacks from backgrounds similar to mine have fared in such institutions. I will also explore some of the pedagogical implications of both their experiences and mine.

The Hump

The public school system I entered in 1957 was a de facto segregated system, one that wasn't working well for Blacks as a whole then and, in fact, one that never had. Consider the following description by Colin Greer (1976):

> The report of the Superintendent of Schools for 1957 showed a drop of 20,000 in the number of white pupils. Negroes then formed a highly concentrated 20.1 percent of the school population. As many as 455 of 704 schools in the city were "homogenous" with less than 10 percent blacks in white schools and vice versa. In 1954 Kenneth Clark argued that the Brown decision be applied to the schools of the North that were segregated by the effects of a combination of neighborhood concentration of Negroes, and neighborhood school zoning. The Board of Education requested the Public Education Association to examine the problem. One year later it reported that in schools of high non-white concentration the children scored below children of other schools in various achievement tests. The school buildings in these districts were older and the proportion of substitute teachers highest.
>
> In 1957 the Board of Education began to keep meticulous ethnic — "black, white, and other" — records on the racial composition of its schools. By this time blacks constituted 25 percent of elementary school pupils and 20 percent of both junior high and vocational high school student bodies. Only 5 percent of the academic high school population was black. Six years later State Commissioner Allen's study of school segregation found the rate of segregation and poor black performance increasing and projected the continuation of the trend. Segregation was virtually synonymous with urban school inadequacy. (pp. 149–50)

That such a system failed Blacks so miserably comes as no surprise to Greer, though he argues that segregation is a reflection of other evils in society, not a cause in and of itself of Black failure in school. Greer's overarching contention is that Blacks are but one in a long line of minority groups that have been denied success within the urban public school community. The treatment they have received has been particularly harsh, but not unique. For the actual social purpose of the public school has long been, Greer states, to fail up to 40 percent of its students. In this view of American educational history the public school is not seen to be a magnificent vehicle for upward mobility, as is the traditional notion; it is viewed instead as a machine that exists to disable students, to remove them from the running for middle-class status, thereby ensuring the maintenance of exploitative social structures. Greer wants us to understand that school identifies those who can accept a strict routinizing of their lives, points out those who can be expected to perform, to know their places. It is seen as a giant sorting operation that helps define for America those students for whom the promise of "getting ahead" will be fulfilled. Those who are slated to live lower-class lives are conditioned to accept their fate and taught how to function in their prescribed roles.

Revisionist historians such as Greer do not claim that this general failure is the result of any personal conspiracy; the assertion, to the contrary, is that it is the product of the social organization of public schools, a network of relations that has inexorably achieved the political task described above regardless of personnel changes. Naturally one may quarrel with Greer's conceptualization. I, for one, favor a more transactional analysis, a focus on the choices certain individuals make when confronted with certain circumstances. Such an approach seems richer to me than the strictly deterministic notion Greer sets forth. Consequently, when assessing school communities I am more apt to speak of their nature than their purpose. But I must admit that whichever lens is used, in this case the object looks pretty much the same: Masses and masses of minority students have been unable to use the public school system as a ladder of upward mobility. It is clear that whatever benefits the school can claim to have offered can be matched, if not overshadowed, by a legacy of default.

Levy, a sociologist, conducted perhaps the most interesting study (1970) relevant to this particular line of thinking. During the 1967–68 school year he went "underground" by taking a teaching job in a ghetto elementary school, fictitiously called Midway, which had an overwhelming Black and Puerto Rican student population. Because Levy was a "floater" (a teacher without regular assignment), he had no trouble conducting the wide range of observations that are summarized below.

The older teachers ("chronic" teachers in Levy's terms) firmly believed that "control must precede education" (p. 25). They spent the great majority of their time and energy as teachers attempting to master the technology of control, a system of devices including bribery, work routines, and even physical violence. In actuality, for the chronic teacher, control did not simply precede education, but was education itself. The younger, more idealistic teachers (the "acute" ones) went to the school feeling that they were morally above such practice and posture. However, when their humanistic overtures were rebuffed, when they were psychologically destroyed by openly rebellious and "disrespectful" students, then they all too happily embraced the chronic teachers' methods and thereby served, too, as agents of control. Many of the acute teachers went to Midway to avoid Vietnam, but the militaristic rigidity they soon adopted would certainly have served them well as soldiers. They paid a high price, however, with their own psychic ambivalence.

While the teachers and students were destroying each other, the students were learning something very crucial: how not to remain eligible for middle-class life. They learned very well how to play their roles as lower-class citizens. Through contact with their White teachers, virtually their only contact with mainstream America, they learned in what terms they would be viewed by the larger society. Or as Levy phrases it: "By the end of the third year, in many classes, education has hardened into open class struggle between teachers and children" (p. 86).

Drawn into this fray were pass-the-buck administrators, thoroughly frustrated and angry parents, and a small number of Black teachers, who experienced the conflicting demands of race and profession. They were most trusted by the students and were thus in a position to betray them most effectively — which they did.

So the ingredients at Midway formed an explosive mix. But as long as the explosions that did occur were contained, the school functioned to, in fact, further suppress. Such a state of affairs led Levy to conclude that "with class politics cloaked in the language of social amelioration, Midway illustrates the contradictions of a society committed to the American dream in a period when that dream is becoming less and less realizable" (p. 176).

For those concerned particularly with language arts instruction, perhaps the most fruitful aspect of the analysis presented by the likes of Greer and Levy is, ironically, that it has nothing at all to say about linguistic or cognitive abilities or disabilities. As mentioned earlier, theirs is a straightforward materialist conception based on the scarcity of resources made available to the masses as a whole, the historical role of Black folks in urban America as a reserve, contingency, or marginal labor force, and the maneuvers of certain interest groups that wish to preserve the status quo. This is important to bear in mind when one hears arguments citing Black language or the inability of Blacks to master Standard English as the major cause of their lack of success in school. One should realize, given the nature of school as it has evolved, that despite any method of instruction per se, the odds have been greatly stacked against many of the Black children who, at the age of five or six, have so optimistically crossed the threshold of public school. It is little wonder that researchers have perceived these children to be entering an educational death trap that in just three or four years practically forces them to abandon their initial enthusiasm for school-based educational life.

Gittin Ovuh, Getting Over

In the city's segregated school system, P.S. 90 on 148th Street was a typical "Black unit," an overwhelmingly Black student population housed in a substandard physical plant staffed by White professionals who, I am sure, would not have minded working somewhere else. Nevertheless, I entered school with little trepidation — certainly none, as the preceding chapter indicates, with respect to my language abilities. Largely through my encounters within the home, I possessed the self-esteem and linguistic skill to participate in a spontaneous, unself-conscious manner among my peers and to feel unintimidated by the mere presence of a White teacher. My first rating on the personality scale used by the Board of Education (see Table 2, in Appendix) included a positive mark in Relationship to Other Children and high marks in Leadership, Self-Confidence, and Initiative. I was also labeled "moderately aggressive" and characterized as one who "occasionally resents group control." Nothing in that personality description of me as a kindergartener predicts any serious problems.

I received virtually the same character assessment for the two months I spent in the first grade at P.S. 90; the only difference was that I was then rated as "responding well to group control." Again, there was no cause for anyone who possessed faith in school to become alarmed. At the age of six I did not feel betrayed by school, had not perceived any hostility being directed at me. I felt, quite to the contrary, very excited about getting on with scientific endeavors.

I landed in school just one month before the Russians launched Sputnik and the space race began in earnest. My fascination with this contest for technological supremacy, an interest no doubt spurred on by the government-induced commitment of the school vigorously to promote science and mathematics teaching (see Perkinson 1977), is another theme evident throughout the narrative. As the story indicates, my base of operations was shifted from Harlem to Queens in November 1958. The most noteworthy aspect of that move for me in education was that the specific nature of the much-postulated hump I would have to try to climb changed radically. Rather than having to endure as a Black student in a segregated Black school, I was going to have to make it as a "minority" student in a predominantly White institution.

Aside from the obvious culture shock I experienced, the major problem I confronted was the opinion that had been formed of me by school officials. I was assigned to 1-4 class as opposed to the 1-1 class that I had been in at P.S. 90. This move was very important inasmuch as the public schools were operating under a multitrack system by that time. In most

instances, students in the *one*-level classes were considered the most capable learners; those in *four* or *five* classes were viewed as relatively slow.
Perkinson claims that such a multitrack arrangement "often proved to be
a 'cover-up' of a highly segregated educational program" (p. 60). I am not
saying that because I was a kid fresh out of Harlem that someone decided
that I was automatically supposed to be slow. What I do know, in retrospect, is that at some point I had to make it to the one-level class to have
my best chance of academic success at P.S. 149.

Of course we know that I made it. After spending less than two months
in 1-4, I was transferred to 1-3, and I was in 2-1 the following September.
This account differs from the one given in "Semivoices." In my recollection I saw myself as always being in the one-level class. But despite this
discrepancy, the essential import of "Semivoices" remains the same. From
the outset of my career at P.S. 149 I displayed enough qualities having
to do with being adept at struggle, with being a confident, moderately
aggressive but cagey competitor.

But the stress of trying to get over the hump at P.S. 149 found some
expression on the personality scale. Several of the ratings I received during
my first three years at the Queens school contrast sharply with the way
I was perceived in Harlem. Although my self-confidence and initiative
were never questioned, my ratings plunged relative to leadership ability
and my relationship with other children. I cannot imagine that I would
have received such marks back up at P.S. 90, not among those with whom
I had so much more in common. I was said not to get along with other
students even *before* I punched the girl in the eye. My teachers in Queens
could not appreciate just how hard I worked to fit in socially or how effec-
tive I actually was at finding a niche that would be acceptable to the class
as a whole.

By the end of third grade, in addition to the marks indicated above,
my occasional resentment of group control and my occasional evading of
responsibility had become constants. Also, that my relationship with my
parents seemed disturbed was duly noted. I guess my teachers were more
accurate in those assessments. Unfortunately, the only conclusion they
drew from them was that I needed "supervision." They were nowhere near
the whole truth about me, which was , in short, that I was showing some
cracks under the strain of all the various role-playing I was engaged in.
Nonetheless, I held myself together enough emotionally to handle the
academic requirements of those one-level classes.

At the close of my third term at P.S. 149, I was classified as satisfactory in reading, writing, and oral communication. That was no spectacular
accomplishment per se, but the way in which it was achieved is what is

most worth considering. It took great social acumen to go from 146th Street in Harlem to a roughly 97 percent White environment in a classroom in Queens and be judged, at the age of nine, as satisfactory in language use. I will examine this movement from a broader perspective.

A Transactional View

My getting over the hump is attributable above all else to the fact that I was able to participate in a series of social deals or transactions that benefited me. There is no way to recount them all, but "Semivoices" indicates the most outstanding and suggests the range these transactions covered.

Relations in the home once again become a point of interest. I argued earlier that it was largely through the supportiveness of my mother and older sister that my language abilities began to flourish and that such support was the chief reason I entered school expecting to succeed. It is clear in "Semivoices" that my father was also a key member of my booster club. Having been deprived of formal educational opportunity, he had extra motive for wishing me only the best in school. Naturally my frantic need to show off on parents' observation day was a way of reassuring him that the best was indeed taking place.

For the same reason I was glad my mother went to that parent-teacher conference. I knew she would see displays of my work. Unfortunately, she was told about my display of temper. Because she heard about the incident long after it occurred, I think my mother's strong reaction to the news was one of fear more than anger. She was afraid I would jeopardize my chances by becoming too great a problem, and she let me know in the best way she knew how that she couldn't allow that to happen.

Despite my mother's obvious concern with my education, she proved to be frequently inaccessible for my direct questioning, no doubt because of the weight of other problems upon her. But I resolved that difficulty fairly well as evidenced by the scene of my moon-sun confusion in which I used my sister to mediate the learning experience. And I kept on stepping. On balance, my familial relations, which I helped establish to some degree, continued to give me the self-confidence in my ability that was noted by every one of my teachers.

The second outstanding deal I was able to strike was with my peers in the classroom. Notwithstanding the black eye fiasco, and partly due to it, I was in good standing in that circle by the close of the third grade and eventually became a frequent and most welcome visitor in several of my classmate's homes. We already know that I went to P.S. 149 armed with some sense of the benefits of code-switching, as my name-switching technique illustrates. But as a result of trying to and then landing such a key position among my classmates I greatly enhanced that set of skills.

Hudson (1980) provides further insight:

> If we think of a child in an area where there are two groups of children of roughly his age, and he belongs clearly to one of them, then he will most probably model his speech largely on that of others in the group he has *chosen*. In other words, at each act of utterance his speech can be seen as an ACT OF IDENTITY in a multi-dimensional space. (p. 14)

My classmates had Raymond's allegiance, and he could communicate much like them. He could not exactly speak like the child of middle-class Jewish parents, but he certainly could avoid sounding like the average kid from Harlem.

The deal I cut with the principal is arguably the highlight of "Semivoices." My skills of impression management were put to, and passed, their stiffest test to that point. I had to appear, as the story depicts, most remorseful, but I couldn't lay the remorse on so thickly that my performance appeared to be too much con. Mr. Price quite naturally could lay a little con himself. I traded him renewed commitment to an agenda for dedication to an image.

My teachers and I hammered out a similar agreement. Although they habitually complained about my talkativeness, I never became a serious acting-out problem, a fact the personality scale is testimony to. And because I handled the curriculum so well, they just about had to put up with me in the one class and expect the same level of achievement from me anticipated of all one-level students. Consequently, I profited from what popularly has been termed the Pygmalion effect, an expectancy process in which the teacher sets high achievement as the "occasion" and the student "rises" to it.

In the original Pygmalion study conducted by Rosenthal and Jacobson (1968), children at a California school, referred to as Oak School, were given a learning ability test. The twenty teachers included in the study were then told that a certain percentage of their students had been identified as "bloomers," children who would show marked improvement during the course of the school year. In reality, no such identification had been made, and the so-called bloomers had been selected at random. Nonetheless, after retesting, the bloomers between ages six and eight showed significant gains in IQ. The notion of the self-fulfilling prophecy had empirical substantiation.

Much controversy has been generated by the Rosenthal and Jacobson study, responses ranging from harsh criticism to an acceptance far more rigid than the data suggest. Subsequent research efforts, possibly because of weaknesses in design, have failed to confirm the effect. Even the original study failed to show this dynamic operative in a majority of cases. However, Colin Rogers (1982), who has specialized in the study of expectancy processes in schools, seems to have approached the matter sensibly.

> It ought to by now be clear that any straightforward conclusion regarding the existence and nature of the teacher-expectancy effect is unlikely to be forthcoming. The studies directly concerned with examining the presence or absence of the effect and those concerned with some of the central aspects of the teacher-expectancy effect show that it is not an all-pervasive phenomenon. It is unlikely to be found in every classroom in every school. By no means could the available data be interpreted so as to suggest that every school-child and every teacher will be directly affected by the operation of a self-fulfilling prophecy. However, it would be reasonable to conclude that every child and every teacher is potentially "at risk." The teacher-expectancy effect is potentially omnipresent if not actually so. This conclusion is sufficient to justify continued examination of the self-fulfilling prophecy within the schools. Furthermore, such future research should no longer continue to attempt to demonstrate the actual existence of the effect. There is now sufficient evidence to show that some pupils at some times will be the victims or beneficiaries of the biasing effects of their teachers' expectations. (p. 167)

Given the environment I was in, I think it is extremely naive to believe that I did not have to conquer some measure of malevolent prejudice and by doing so I profited from a benevolent type.

A fifth vitally important transaction, one that won't be considered at length just yet, was worked out with the community, particularly my blood brother. No matter what aspirations I held and achieved along with Whites, I can honestly say that I never had any conscious longing to *be* White. I never wished to trade my background or culture. Remember, I was a lover of Eighth Avenue. My blood brother could understand all the Black things about me and share with me a special camaraderie. Both he and the community at large have had their say in how this entire work has taken shape.

I hope by this point to have dispelled all conceptions that early elementary school progress is most appropriately explained as the maturation of some genetic gift or exposure to some success-stamping curriculum. Genetic predispositions are little understood, but what is certain is that, whatever they are, they must be expressed in a social world, a world of negotiation. Exploring the scope of social relations in an educational world will yield the most veridical understanding of educational progress. As for the curriculum referred to here, it was the same as that in place, with mixed results, all over the city. There was no magic in it.

Looking back at the early years, I find it impossible to recommend that African-American students be asked to follow in my footsteps, to leave the onus almost entirely on them to fit in, to hope they can pull together a similar but just as improbable combination of pacts in order to accomplish the task of language learning in school. As mentioned previously, even with the success I was achieving, my complex juggling act was a tremendous strain on me. And although it is correct to view third grade as a critical juncture, we will see that there were major hurdles yet to face. So if I criticize elements of the school system, let it not be said that I am being ungrateful. I learned a lot, but I had to foot the psychic bill for any success I managed to attain. Surely, in one sense, the consumer is always right.

Eradicationism, Pluralism, and Bidialectalism

The situation of most African-American students concerning formal language instruction can be analyzed in terms of eradicationism, pluralism, or bidialectalism expressed in institutional policy and/or the actions of individual teachers. When pondering the best approach to instructing these students, it is important, therefore, to consider the relative merits of these views.

Eradicationists believe that Standard English is the only language variety that has a legitimate function within the school. In their judgment Black English is not only inappropriate, but is indicative of minimal intelligence or cognitive deficiency. They may cite researchers such as Bereiter and Engelmann (1966) and Jensen (1969) to back their claims. From their outlook poor reading and writing scores by Black English speakers are understood to be the direct result of these students' inability to abandon their own delimiting dialect. Some eradicationists want these students to receive instruction before they even show up at school. As erasing Black dialect is a worthwhile aim, the reasoning goes, the earlier such treatment is initiated the better off the speaker of that dialect will be. After all, they ask, since other minorities (usually meaning European immigrants) readily took to Standard English and subsequently progressed, why shouldn't Blacks be expected to do the same thing? Some eradicationists even contend that other elements of Black culture should be discarded as well — all, of course always, for the students' benefit.

Kozol ran headlong into eradicationism in process within the Boston public school system. The repression, frustration, and anger he encountered are not untypical of how such a concept is manifested in reality. Among other abuses, including strict control over whatever writing they managed to squeeze out, the students were exposed to a most uninspiring reading program, expected to wrestle with books they could neither relate to nor enjoy. Kozol describes the predicament:

> [F]or nothing could better typify the image of the crumbling school structure than the dry and deadly basic reading textbooks that were in use within my school. . . . The volume aimed at Third Graders, used for slow Fourth Graders at my school, was called *New Streets and Roads*. No title could have been farther from the mark. Every cliche of bad American children's literature seemed to have been contained within this book. The names of the characters describe the flavor of the stories: Betty Jane Burns and Sarah Best and Miss Molly and Fluffy Tail and Miss Valentine of Maple Grove School. . . . The children in my class had been hearing already for several years about Birmingham and Selma and tear-gas and cattle-prods and night-courts and slum-lords—and jazz. To expect these children to care about books which even very comfortable suburban children would probably have found irrelevant and boring seemed to be futile. (p. 79)

Kozol introduced material the children found relevant and stimulating. But he was eventually terminated for this action, specifically for teaching Langston Hughes's "Ballad of the Landlord." The following is Kozol's account of a statement by the Deputy Superintendent.

> Miss Sullivan's statement on my dismissal was much the same as Mr. Ohren-berger's [the Superintendent's], adding, however, a general admonition about the dangers of reading to Negro children poems written in bad grammar. Although Langston Hughes "has written much beautiful poetry," she said, "we cannot give directives to the teachers to use literature written in native dialects." It was at this time that she made the statement to which I have alluded earlier: "We are trying to break the speech patterns of these children, trying to get them to speak properly. This poem does not present correct grammatical expression and would just entrench the speech patterns we want to break." (p. 204)

Such a supercilious commitment to eradicationism ignored the facts that (a) children generally do not talk like poems, (b) the dialect was already entrenched, and (c) teaching the poem was a real educational success. To hear from Kozol once again:

> I also think it ought to be taken seriously by a teacher when a group of young children come in to him one morning and announce that they have liked something so much that they have memorized it voluntarily. It surprised me and impressed me when that happened. It was all I needed to know to confirm for me the value of reading that poem and the value of reading many other poems to children which will build upon, and not attempt to break down, the most important observations and very deepest foundations of their lives. (p. 165)

Although the events reported above epitomize "Black units" in Boston's de facto segregated school system circa 1965, there is much evidence that eradicationist practices have always been on display in numerous institutions attended by Blacks, regardless of racial distribution. Legal action in the celebrated King case, for example, was initiated on behalf of fifteen children who attended a school at which only 13 percent of the students were Black. It is interesting to note that the furor generated by the case along with the subsequent criticism of Judge Joiner's decision demonstrate that the eradicationist impulse in the nation is still strong. A clear example of this is "What's Wrong with Black English," an article by Rachel Jones (1982).

The best thing I can say about eradicationism is that it is definitely wrong and has never actually worked. Certainly nothing in the modern body of sociolinguistic theory gives even the slightest credence to the strategy. Trudgill (1974) informs us that

> Linguists, and many others, believe this approach to be wrong, for several reasons. First, it is wrong *psychologically.* Language, as we have seen, is not simply a means of communicating messages. It is also very important as a symbol of identity and group membership. To suggest to a child that his language, and that of those with whom he identifies, is inferior in some way is to imply that *he* is inferior. This, in turn, is likely to lead either to alienation from the school and school values, or to a rejection of the group to which he belongs. It is also *socially* wrong in that it may appear to imply that particular social groups are less valuable than others. This is particularly undesirable when the language being stigmatized is that of lower-class black children and the one which is being extolled is that of white middle-class adult teachers. Finally, and perhaps most importantly, it is *practically* wrong: it is wrong because it does not and will not work. . . . The fact must also be faced that, in very many cases, speakers will not *want* to change their language — even if it were possible. (pp. 80–81)

Pluralists insist that the language of Blacks be left alone since it is as good as any other. While it is true, these critics assert, that Black English speakers suffer setbacks in the society at large, such setbacks are due to who they are — not what they speak. As Sledd (1973) opines, "but in job-hunting in America, pigmentation is more important that pronunciation" (p. 212).

An experiment by Frederick Williams (1973) fuels the argument that racial prejudice overrides concerns of linguistic output. Separate videotapes were made of three children: Black, White, and Mexican-American. Enough of the children was visible so that racial characteristics were apparent, but the children had been filmed at such an angle that a viewer could not see the movement of their mouths as they spoke. The same voiceover was then dubbed onto all the tapes. Nonetheless, when student teachers were asked to rate the children's speech for standardness and fluency, the White child's speech was rated superior. It seems foolish to dispute the belief of Burling (1973) that "when we are contemptuous of a people, we tend to be contemptuous of their language" (p. 20), even if what they are speaking is really our own.

Pluralists may compliment the sociolinguistic sophistication of Switzerland, where quadralingualism is officially established; they may praise the sensitivity of the German public school system for its adroit handling of dialect differences (see Fishman and Leuders-Salmon 1972). Or they may vigorously denounce American education, forging, in essence, a language-oriented extension of the Greer-Levy critique. O'Neil (1973) pursues that line of thought.

> How then does language education — without, remember, worrying about the motivations of individual teachers, school administrators, or textbook makers — fit into this analysis? On this analysis it follows that the enterprise of making lower-class speakers over into middle-class speakers is simply a piece of the educational emptiness that helps maintain the present distribution of power in society. For wasting time there, on a thing that is bound to fail, serves to render school children skilled enough to be exploited but finally uneducated, used to failure, and alienated enough not to oppose exploitation; thus for them to continue to agree that they had their chances to succeed in a free and open society but that they failed. No one's fault but their own. (pp. 189–90)

Concerning the immigrant-success fallacy, a favorite one among eradicationists, pluralists will agree that the means by which any progress was achieved is unlikely to appeal to the majority of Black children. They concur with Fader:

> Children of white immigrants knew they had only to assume the clothing of the dominant group — in large part, its language — and they could live undetected in its midst. Knowing that lifelong masquerade to be beyond them — being so informed by the shape of everything from the obelisk of the Washington monument to the rectangle of a television box — black and brown children see no reason for wearing clothes that give them neither warmth nor camouflage. (pp. 116–17)

To the pluralist the crucial work involving language education is to develop a school system (and of course a society) in which language differences fail to have deleterious consequences for those whose language has been traditionally frowned upon. The proposal is not to ignore Standard Enlgish. One would certainly teach all children to read it. But beyond that the feeling is that in a more equitable societal arrangement or in a subenvironment pursuing that goal, Black students will be not only more inclined to see the value of expanding their productive communicative repertoires, but prove rather skillful at accomplishing the task.

Bidialectalists postulate that Black English is equal to Standard English but not quite equal enough. They acknowledge that the language variety is not inferior linguistically or conceptually but, claiming to be pragmatic, they feel that Standard English must be mastered by Black children in the schools so that these children can keep the possibility of upward mobility alive. Bidialectalists would rally around the argument of Baratz (1969) that "since standard English is the language of the mainstream it seems clear that knowledge of the mainstream system increases the likelihood of success in the mainstream culture" (p. 76). Beyond such general assent, however, the bidialectalists defy stereotyping. They range from thinly disguised eradicationists to would-be pluralists blocked by a lack of commitment. But pluralists, who view a policy of bidialectalism, like eradicationism, as a tool of subjugation, are uncompromisingly critical of even those at the latter end of the continuum. As Smitherman espouses, "teaching strategies which seek only to put white middle-class English into the mouths of black speakers ain did nothin to inculcate the black perspective necessary to address the crises in the black community" (p. 209).

The concepts of eradicationism, pluralism, and bidialectalism undoubtedly will be tossed around and debated for some time to come, with sparks flying. It should be obvious, however, that the pluralist notion is correct and is the only one in this day and age to which the majority of Black children are likely to subscribe. Eradicationism is surely wrong and at any rate impossible unless the children themselves are eliminated. Being bidialectal can certainly be a valuable skill. But people don't become bidialectal just because someone thinks it's a good idea. They mostly sell themselves on the need to be bidialectal. It's a matter beyond curriculum.

Social relations are a far more vital factor for Black students in school than differences of language variety. Black children, like all people, make decisions based on vested interests. If they were to perceive that the social dialectic were in their favor, learning another dialect could not be a major problem. In fact it would be extremely difficult to *prevent* them from learning Standard English. For most Blacks in school such perception can form only within a setting in which teachers genuinely accept them as they come and respect them enough not to sell them myths of simple assimilation. The worst thing any of us can do, who have bought such myths for however long, is to pretend the package was always an easy one to carry home.

6
Big Fame
and Other Games

I

One of the first things Mrs. Kaufmann wanted to know was how her class of nine year olds was responding to the era of space exploration. She wanted poems for the bulletin board on this theme. I had never tried writing any poetry before, but I figured I could do it if I wanted to. So after a brief moment of thought and deciding on the rather unimaginative title "Space Poem," I hacked out my first stanza:

A trip to Mars
Is like one to the stars,
A place to go
And a place you don't know.

Dumb, sure, but I was in step. And I took my reader on a wondrous tour of the galaxy before winding down with:

But no matter how far I roam
I'll always want to come back home,
Where the atmosphere is always glad
With my three sisters and Mom and Dad.

I was satisfied with the effort; there was no problem with rhyming; I felt I had a decent poem. Mrs. Kaufmann agreed. I was standing at her desk as she removed her glasses and cast her long black hair over her shoulders.

"This is good work Raymond" she said softly. "I'm going to use it for the bulletin board."

"Thank you Mrs. Kaufmann." I couldn't think of anything further to say.

"You have a fine rhythmic sense. Did you know that?"

"No Mrs. Kaufmann. I don't think rhyming words is all that hard."

"Rhyme is something altogether different" she smiled. "I'm speaking now of rhythm, of the flow of words, of the syllable count, the stresses, the beat. I'm talking about the beat. Do you understand what I'm saying?"

"Yes. I think I do. More or less."

"Do you count the syllables Raymond?"

"No Mrs. Kaufmann, I just go by how it sounds. If it sounds all right I leave it. If it doesn't, then maybe I'll change a word or two."

"Weren't you aware of the fact that you were groping for rhythm?"

"No. Not really. Like I said, I just go by how it sounds." She put her glasses back on and fidgeted with them until they were just right. Kept a constant eye on me.

"Do you like poetry Raymond?"

"It's okay I guess. I never tried writing any before."

"Well maybe you can develop your ability. You should practice more. And read more too. Do you have a library card?"

"Yes I have one. I've had one for a long time."

"That's good. . . . On your next trip to the library be sure to look up Langston Hughes and Ogden Nash. You might like them. Should I write the names down, or can you remember?"

Langston and Ogden, how could I forget? And I found that Ogden could keep me laughing with his zany rhymes as he satirized everything from nicknames to advertising slogans. Langston made me laugh also as he satirized everything from funerals to freedom. But Langston would slip in some somber thoughts about funerals and freedom that I didn't fully understand. So I figured I had to keep laughing with him for the time being and catch on to the other stuff further on down the line, when I got big.

I thought poetry writing might be a good hobby, maybe even as good as space study itself. But, by then, both had to take a back seat to athletics. That became the undying compulsion and I played and observed all I possibly could. The moments were unfolding that would become the central core of my sports memory, visions I can recall more readily and with more exactness than many events of far more recent times. Naturally there were the boys in pinstripes. And Mickey, who might have been the greatest if he could have kept his legs off the operating table. Well there were all sorts of injuries, really, and there was blood oozing from a wound in his butt, blood staining the seat of his uniform as he lashed a wicked liner off the scoreboard in Crosley Field and limped to first base. There was Wilt the Stilt averaging 50.4 points per game and tossing in 100 one night against the Knicks. And Elgin Baylor, the greatest forward of them all. There were men called Katcavage, Robustelli, Webster, Rote, Gifford, Barnes, and Y.A. Tittle rolling up big victories on Sundays. And there was Del Shofner, on a bitterly cold day at Soldiers Field, dropping a sure touchdown pass in the end zone as the Giants blew the title to the Bears. There were Sugar Ray Robinson and Gene Fullmer and my biggest childhood hero of them all — Sonny Liston.

Sonny would bring those massive fourteen-inch fists directly to the center of the ring, fix his menacing scowl just right, and then swat his opponent down. And I loved it. Lots of people talked bad about Sonny in an attempt to discourage my admiration, but this only strengthened my adulation. Sure I knew Sonny was considered a thug and all, but I also knew he could knock out three guards at one time in the jailhouse. You see, Sonny had what most men wanted: a big reputation. That was important.

When he bombed Patterson in the first round in Chicago to gain the crown and then bombed him again in the first round in Las Vegas to retain it, I was simply overjoyed. But Floyd was so embarrassed that he began sneaking around in phony moustaches and disguises like that, which was something I couldn't understand. Floyd had done his best so, according to my father, he had nothing to be ashamed of. I didn't think an athlete, a hero, should have to wear a mask.

For a time I belonged almost exclusively to 149 playground. Had to put down Junction Park because it was too small for football and softball and only had two hoops. Lonnie Blair played sports in spots, mostly handball. He stayed around Junction Park or up at 92. He thought I was foolish for wanting to play it all. I thought he was foolish for wanting to miss any, a single odd roll of the football. I had to have it all, and it became a problem.

One day in early December I persuaded several of my classmates to join me in challenging a group of fifth and sixth graders to a game of two-handed touch after school. When our challenge was accepted I was excited because it meant a rare chance for me to get some real competition. My classmates were fun, but things had already reached the point where I had to coast when playing against them in order to keep our games interesting. There wasn't a single one of them who could get two hands on me in the open field, and there wasn't one I couldn't track down with ease. My side always had a sure win, but I kept it close. No need, however, to coast against the older boys. I had been watching them play regularly and knew we didn't have much of a chance. Which meant it would be up to me to create one.

At dismissal time I was so eager I quickly vaulted from my seat, only to bang my right knee hard against the side railing. It wasn't the first time I had done it but it was certainly the worst time. I must have banged that knee at the worst possible angle or something, just couldn't shake the pain. We got slaughtered in the game. And there was this guy named Bennett who put the tag on me at every turn. Whenever I got the ball, grimaced, and tried one of my Ernie Davis moves, he slapped on the tag easily and laughed tauntingly, "Ha. I thought you were supposed to be so good."

After the game I limped home and began rubbing alcohol on the painful joint. It was so swollen it alarmed the usually placid Sherry.

"That thing looks terrible . . . nasty. A whole sea of alcohol wouldn't help that knee."

"You don't know what a sea would do" I snapped. "All we got is this bottle. It'll be good enough."

"Hmph. That's what you think. You wait."

Sherry was right. I used the whole bottle and didn't feel any better. I decided to try to catch Pops upstairs. Luckily he was in, and I hobbled into his room with my pants leg rolled up.

"I need some money for some alcohol for my knee." He looked at the joint and winced as though it hurt him also.

"You been walkin around on that? What happened?"

"I banged it on the desk in school."

"Runnin and actin wild I bet. I'll lay odds on that." Then he asked sternly, "Were you?"

"No" I answered sharply. "I was just getting out of my seat and it just happened. I wasn't fooling around or anything like that."

"That knee looks too bad to have just happened." But he didn't press the issue, merely stated calmly, "Well you sure don't need no alcohol. We need to check this thing out at a hospital."

It was found that I had a multiple fracture of the patella. In other words, a cracked kneecap. I thought this would get me a cast similar to the one Michael Stein had when he broke his leg skiing. But instead a nurse wheeled me upstairs and dumped me in a bed.

"But where's my cast?" I asked my father in protest.

"I don't know about no cast. I guess you won't be gettin one."

"Well what are they gonna do to me? They have to do something."

"Oh they'll do somethin all right."

"But what?"

"Make you feel better."

"How?"

"By takin care of that knee for you."

"Yeah but they're supposed to put a cast on it and they're not."

"Maybe they don't need to in this case. They might have to figure out somethin else."

"But WHAT?" I was just about at the panic stage.

"Can't tell you that son. You being a patient all of a sudden don't make me no doctor all of a sudden. They'll get everything straight. Just relax. Take it easy."

Turned out the doctors weren't too sure about what to do themselves. I heard something about a possible operation, something else about a possible draining of fluids. All I knew for sure, however, was that I was lying with my leg in traction virtually all day and night, running a hell of a fever, and taking plenty of needles in tender places.

My mother showed up nearly every day after work with the newspaper, maybe some magazines, and more fruit than I could ever handle. She would finger the knee ever so gingerly and relate stories from home. I always asked first about Debra Lynn.

My father would show up, at other times of course, with sports magazines and even more fruit. We talked mainly about football. It was almost time for him to slip down the stairs and out the door for good.

I spent most of my time in the hospital gazing out of the window, often counting bricks on the adjacent wing. Sometimes demolishing the building with my imagination. Sometimes reconstructing it. Sometimes modifying it, making it slightly taller but narrower, or shorter but wider.

I worried about my mother a lot. Wondered if she could stay so solid. She had super moments, but she was no superwoman type. Couldn't handle every big thing and every little thing too. Even back then she would load me, specifically, with responsibility, expect much of me. No overprotection. No simple matriarchal stuff with me. Naturally we had our battles over priorities, over power. But overall, she was a pretty good designer of futures.

The nurses were nice, but I felt overly self-conscious about using the bed pan. Just figured no nurse really wanted to do that job. I would withstand severe stomach cramps far longer than I should have, repeatedly denying the need for the pan, until I would finally break down and request it. And I would read off and on, no real concentration, and give away most of my fruit to other patients who stopped by to visit. I read the card from my classmates over and over again and it always said the same thing: You are sorely missed. Of course I already knew that I was sore, but missed, well, that was nice to hear. And then on the 23rd, as my fear of being confined on Christmas was peaking, I was allowed to go home.

I was preparing to hop down from the bed when my father's voice caused me to hesitate. "Wait Keith. They're gonna take you down in a wheelchair."

"A wheelchair? Not me. I don't need no wheelchair." I hopped to my feet and promptly collapsed, would have hit the floor hard if not for my father's quick reflexes.

"Ain't no need to get hardheaded now boy."

"You mean I really can't walk?" I asked incredulously.

"You'll be all right in a little while. Just have to get your balance back. Can't stay off your feet for weeks and just hop up and scoot around. Takes a few minutes. Gotta get readjusted."

I went home to learn to walk for the second time in my life, and Sherry spoiled Christmas in a way by telling me she knew she was getting a radio. I suspected I would get one also since we both had received watches the year before. My guess was correct and, though there was no moment of surprise, there was a moment of happiness as the holidays rolled on and we kicked out another year on the front steps.

I closed out the school year in pretty decent fashion. Only major problem had been that I had left most of my language arts workbook blank. Mrs. Kaufmann didn't check them regularly, and it was easy to take liberties. Whenever my turn came during class review, I simply read aloud the answer I would have written if I had bothered to do the exercise. One day, however, Mrs. Kaufmann did decide to check. I can't remember if it was just on general principle or whether she had caught someone else faking it. That part is a little fuzzy, but it's clear what happened to me. I was run over quickly by the Kaufmann-to Sherry-to Moms express. Had to shake the pain off, drag myself back together, and spend an entire evening confined to my room as I made up the work. The only consolation was that I secretly caught a Yankees game on the radio.

I had written a poem about my latest heroes, John Glenn and Scott Carpenter, and received my standard report card, mostly "goods" and "excellents." But although Mrs. Kaufmann could appreciate my poetry, she didn't enjoy my chattering, which had heightened considerably, and she gave me only a "fair" in conduct. She scribbled in red ink that "Raymond could use more self-control."

My mother said my behavior had better improve the next term. Actually, the threat she made was rather emphatic. I began thinking that I would absolutely and positively improve. But I knew I wouldn't.

II

In September, school started smoothly for me but not for James Meredith. Outside of my family, no one was too concerned that I was in 5-1, but there were many people upset over the fact that Meredith wished to become the first Negro to enroll in the University of Mississippi. Marches and demonstrations by White folks. Countermarches and counterdemonstrations by Negroes. Shotgun ambushes by White folks. Marches and demonstrations by Negroes.

"Wouldn't hafta go that far to keep me from goin to school" commented Lonnie Blair, who was moving from four class to four class. "All they'd hafta do is ask. Would you go Keith?"

"Nah, not me Lonnie. Even *I* don't like school that much."

"Good thing you don't. Cause if you did you'd be kinda dumb."

"I know. Still, those people shouldn't be prejudiced down there."

"Yeah but you know how it is. That's how they be."

That's all the moral support Meredith could get from us two ten year olds. But a few weeks later I was able to get a striking adult view of this and other situations when I was ordered to the barbershop.

As I reluctantly came through the door, Mr. Horton waved me up into his chair. "How you son? Your father said you was comin by today. I see you done let it git nappy enough, don't you think?"

"Yeah I guess so . . . How's business in general Mr. Horton?" My father always asked him that question.

"Slow Tuesday son, that's all, slow Tuesday." He tied the apron around me and reached for a comb. A man in a suit rose, with the help of a cane, from the other chair. He brushed loose hairs away with his left hand, and as he extended to his full height I could see that his right leg was several inches shorter than the other. Besides that he seemed to be in real good shape. He pulled a bill from his pocket, turned it over to Boone and told him to keep the change. Boone looked as if he was trying to save up for a haircut of his own. I mean I had never seen a barber as sloppy about his hair as he was. He wore the first and wildest afro I ever saw. Had a scraggly beard and sideburns. He certainly wasn't such a good advertisement but was, in fact, a good barber. Lots of people asked for Boone. Boone or Horton, didn't make me any difference. Not for the close shave I had to get. Just be fast.

Boone began brushing his customer's clothes with the whisk broom. Then he added, "Thank you Shortside. Appreciate it."

"Ain't nothin Boone, my good man. You know it ain't nothin but a drop." He stretched his left arm out to the side as he started to yawn. When he composed himself again he announced his leave. "Well I got my haircut now. Let me go on and finish sprucin up for the evenin."

"You do that" said Boone. "You take care."

"Yes Mr. Shortside" intruded Mr. Horton. "You watch out for them women."

"Watch out for em? Now Horton, you know I can handle the young ladies. Man, you shoulda seen me the other night." Mr. Shortside had come alive with agitation. "Man, I had this sweet young thing up in the apartment. We naked and she done got me all worked up and everything and then she wants to sit on the edge of the bed and all of a sudden play shy. She was wonderin if she could play for some big money I guess. Says she wanna discuss matters. Can you dig that? 'Discuss matters.' I git a little mad but I don't let on, you know. Can't let the chick have the satisfaction of thinkin she can git next to me like that. I just puts the intelligence in my head. I carries it around in my socks, only got a little bit and I needs to save it like that. So anyway I puts it in my head and then I realize that all I gotta do is keep my cool and use a little indifference myself, you know, like I could take it or leave it myself. And let me tell you somethin. It wasn't long before her mind got off the discussin and back to the bustin. Oh she had a little somethin to say about lookin for real love and all that. But I convinced her that the real love couldn't start until she shut her damn mouth. And I layed it on her too. I ain't got no handicap like that." Mr. Shortside paused briefly to savor whatever the memory was, then switched his tone to one of mock complaint. "Now I can't git rid of the chick. It done even got to where I'm actually duckin her now. Girl trying to be on me tight as a orange peel be on a orange. She gittin peeled though, better believe that."

Boone had been simmering with laughter. Now he boiled. Mr. Horton uttered a restrained "heh heh heh" and continued to comb my hair, me amused all the while. Mr. Shortside grinned, having played his audience well. He then directed his attention my way.

"You a handsome nuff boy, be able to git on it one day like ol Shortside. Can't promise you'll be good as me, but you bound to have just as much fun anyway."

"This Gil's boy here" cut in Mr. Horton. "You know the tall fella be in here, crazy about the Giants like us?"

"Yeah yeah yeah. I know him. Good man . . . You know, I was kinda thinkin this here boy reminded me of somebody I knew. Gil, hunh? This the boy got to be crazy about those Yankees then? Is that so young fella?"

"Uh hunh."

"Well you really don't think they can take this World Series, do you?"

"Uh hunh. I do. They'll beat San Francisco." That answer didn't sit well with Mr. Shortside, so he dismissed it.

"Well every fella got his own weakness, ain't he Horton?"

"You're right about that Shortside. But he's just a kid. He can't remember anything about when the Giants were here in New York." Mr. Shortside studied my face, like it was hard to figure I was only nine or ten.

"I reckon you're right about that Horton. But tell me somethin young fella, you do know about prejudice, don't you?"

"Uh hunh. I know about it." I was ready to listen to an anti-Yankees speech such as the ones my mother gave, but Mr. Shortside came from another direction.

"Well what is it then?" he demanded.

"It's, um, it's, uh, I mean it's like when they didn't want that man in Mississippi to go to school."

"Why it sure is" he responded with surprise. "Gil say he ain't got no dumb boy, and he ain't either. Hey Boone, before I go why don't you tell me and the kid all about the University of Mississippi? Is it truly the University OF Mississippi or not?"

"Aw go on Shortside" Boone laughed. "Why you wanna go back into that? I thought you was talkin baseball."

"Well baseball ain't the whole ballgame, if you dig what I'm sayin. So come on and philosophize for me and the kid." Then he turned to ask me another question. "You didn't know Boone was a philosopher, did you?"

Actually I did. But his main topic on the Saturday mornings when I was usually around was the women who had made him angry.

Boone sat in the barber's chair and propped his feet up on the metal footrest. Stuck his hands into the large pockets of his light blue shirt-jacket. "Well I'll tell ya" he began. "It's OF Mississippi because Negroes are now included in the chance to go there, but it's OF Mississippi because they gonna catch all kinds of hell for really tryin to do it. So it's OF Mississippi and it's good, and it's OF Mississippi and it's bad. And then you can say that it ain't really the University OF Mississippi at all because a Negro might can use that school to get a job opportunity just like a White boy, and that definitely wouldn't represent what Mississippi is all about. So it is and it is and it ain't. All depends on how you look at it."

"Hear that son?" Mr. Shortside would not allow a lull. "Wanna know what all that philosophizin means?"

I certainly did. Up to that point I had only thought that the name of a school was the name of a school. That's all.

"Well do you?"

"Yes I do."

"Then I'll tell you. It means the stuff is so screwed up. Usually when you hear a whole buncha jumbled up philosophy, it means somethin real screwed up is goin on. You git halfway confused tryin to explain the shit. Ain't that right Boone?"

"Yeah Shortside. You ain't far off base puttin it like that. There's always something wrong when those funny explanations come up. Like some folks say he shoulda went wherever he was wanted, while other folks say he shoulda been wanted wherever he went."

"That's right son" beamed Mr. Shortside. "And let me tell you, course you gotta 'cuse my French, that what it all comes down to is that a muthafuckin cracker just don't mean a nigguh no good. It's in the skin, son. It's definitely in the skin. Don't let nobody never tell you that it *ain't* in the skin. And it's the same thing South or North. Ain't a whole lotta difference. Just like I see Kennedy done got this fair housing bill passed, but it don't mean nothin to the people right over here down the street in Honkieville. The bill shoulda been written on toilet tissue cause that's the amount of respect the average cracker gonna give it. Ain't it like that Horton?" Mr. Shortside was pacing now. Handling his cane very well. Moving far swifter than I had thought him capable.

"I think you're right on it" replied Horton.

"Yeah I knows I am. Man with smark socks can't be no all the time fool. Helluva a situation we in, ain't it Boone?"

"Sure is. This a funny country we tryin to call our own."

"Damn right. Helluva funny country. I wouldn't care if Uncle Sam and Baldy Red blowed this whole mother up as long as they let me and a few of those pretty young gals live."

"Now sir" Mr. Horton began laughingly. "Is that all you want from the whole deal?"

"Yeah Horton. Why not? Ain't nothin better to live for. Not how I'm lookin at it now."

Mr. Shortside and Boone became very special in my eyes. They gave the current events much better than Mrs. Holtzman did. More analysis and fervor. My teacher stayed more on the side of soft regret and subdued hope. Whereas she was detached, they had definite points of view.

There hadn't been much spoken about race relations in our home. Only when Moms spoke out against the Yankees. We were never taught to hate White people as a whole. Of course I had always managed to hate them enough for Lonnie Blair. Now I had to ponder whether or not I could despise them enough for my newest mentors, who were taking matters to a new level.

I studied my classmates even more closely. Particularly zoomed in on Michael Stein as we had become pretty solid companions ever since the treaty fiasco back in '60. He and I would recruit other classmates to his home for games of Monopoly and Stratego. Because I had the latest curfew, I could always stay later than any of the others. Many times I would be on hand to greet his parents, who always seemed glad to see me, as they came in from work. And Marcia Stein, Michael's seventeen-year-old sister, seemed especially fond of me, always laughing when I beat Michael at Monopoly and asking me questions about the one class. She usually wanted me to stick around for dinner, even said she was insisting. But I wouldn't. Whenever she popped the question I would glance at my watch and announce that I had to hurry home. I wasn't comfortable enough to sit at their table yet. Besides, I felt my pace was steady enough.

Then there was Marty Rosenberger. He was a real underdog at times, a clumsy sort who could barely walk and hold his pants up at the same time. But he was highly spirited and hustled hard in every sport we played. I always chose him for my team, always bolstered his self-confidence in order to combat his clumsiness, and we got along fine.

The first time I made a prolonged visit to his home was on a Saturday. We were going to watch the basketball game featuring Providence College and Jimmy Walker, who they were billing as the next Oscar Robertson. I raced up to the Southridge Co-ops, excited about his game and mine. As I came off the elevator, Marty was coming out into the hall carrying a bag of garbage. He let the door slam behind him.

"The lock is off Raymond. You can go on in. We have free run of the place."

"All right Marty, game is just about on, isn't it?"

"They're introducing the lineups. Go ahead. Just take your sneakers off before you step on the carpet. It was just done."

His words stunned me for a moment because I had on some air-conditioned socks. You know the style. They weren't all that bad as ragged socks go. Lonnie Blair wouldn't have given them a second thought. But I needed a perfect pair for Marty Rosenberger.

I shot a quick look at Marty nearing the incinerator. Fortunately it was toward the other end of the hall. Slow and clumsy as Marty was, I knew I had a chance. I hurried inside, took my sneakers off without bothering with the laces, and dashed wildly into Marty's room. The second dresser drawer I opened was the correct one, and I changed into a perfect pair of white sweat socks about as quickly as it can be done. The fit was pretty good. I stuffed my own socks into a pocket of my jacket and bolted out into the living room, beating Marty by several seconds. This wasn't quite what Mr. Shortside meant by "smart socks." But in my own way I was learning.

I accepted invitations to their birthday parties, joined the Cub Scouts with them, pack 325. Anything to observe. I watched them in the library down on 82nd Street. While I would delve more into my poets and sports heroes like Joe Louis and Jim Thorpe, they would be more into Anne Frank, thereby influencing my own future reading list. Anything to stay on top of the situation.

One afternoon after a touch football game Michael, Marty, and I were left sitting on a park bench.

"I think I'm getting better now" Marty asserted.

"You are better" I instantly assured him. "You hang on to the ball better now and you're not afraid of the hard passes. Keep it up and you'll be better than me one day."

"I doubt it Raymond." So did I. But like I said, I always did this sort of thing with Marty.

"Don't doubt it Marty. Practice makes perfect and that's all you have to do. You too Michael. You can get a whole lot better also."

"I guess so. But it's only football. My dad says brains are better than brawn."

"Brains *are* better than brawn" I promptly retorted. It was an old debate for us and I was ready to win it convincingly this time. "But that's only if you have to choose one over the other. Having brains *and* brawn is the best you can do. And anyway, catching passes isn't brawn; it's skill. Brawn and skill are different."

"Yeah? Well my dad says that school is more important than all of that. He wants me to do exceptionally well so I can make it all the way to medical school. I know I'll be a doctor. I just don't know my specialty yet. What about you Marty?"

"I think I'll be an accountant or something. As long as the money is good. I won't accept anything under $200 a week. My dad says that's the least he would work for."

This was back when a yearly salary of $10,000 was a very big deal. I knew my father wasn't even halfway to that figure. Not toiling in that machine shop.

"What about you Raymond?" asked Michael abruptly. "What are you going to do?"

"Well I haven't really decided yet" I countered without hestitation. "I can be a lot of things. I might be a football player, a smart one. Or I might be some kind of scientist, or engineer. Or a doctor or an accountant also. No telling what I might end up doing. World may blow up before we get to be adults anyway. You know how they keep talking about World War III."

"Don't say that Raymond."

"Aw I'm just kidding around Michael. Don't be so scary. It won't happen."

"I hope not. But it is possible, isn't it? My dad says Krushchev is a very dangerous man. Calls him the Red Hitler."

"He is bad" Marty cut in. "But nobody's quite as bad as Hitler. There's nobody as bad as somebody who exterminated six million people. That's like killing most of this whole city. If Germany had won the war, Michael, we'd be in concentration camps right now. We might even be dead. He probably wouldn't bother you Raymond. You'd be sorta lucky to be a Negro."

"Man are you crazy? He hated Negroes too."

"You sure about that?"

"Of course I'm sure. Don't be so dumb Marty. I know he hated Jesse Owens for winning all those gold medals at the 1936 Olympics. And I know he hated Joe Louis for knocking the hell out of Max Schmeling. Tell him Michael. Ask your dad about all that. He hated Negroes just as much as he hated Jews."

"I have to check on that" Michael said cautiously. "Maybe he did hate Negroes also, but it must have been a little different from how he hated Jews. He would get us first for sure. Right Marty?"

Naturally Marty agreed with him. I never would, though it wasn't an argument I would press. I knew Jews caught plenty hell. But of course I knew Black folks caught plenty hell too. Some of it from Jews.

We had one of our standard games going on, and Leonard Landau, Barry Weinstein, Mark Greenberg, Marty, and I were one touchdown up on Michael, John Levy, Barry Goldberg, Mark Friedman, and Jerry Weissman. Jerry was running out to catch a pass and I was right with him. Our bodies bumped together slightly and as I stumbled a bit Jerry made the catch and started sprinting down the sideline toward a score. As I was recovering my stride I was thinking about whether I should let him go on and tie the game. A tie was always interesting. Made everything seem more heroic. But I decided not to let Jerry do it. He was the kind of guy who would brag too much if he scored a touchdown on me. I was aware that he resented me a lot because he realized he would have been the best if I weren't around. No, I couldn't allow him to score on me. Michael or Marty, yes, but definitely not Jerry. So I tracked him down and put a firm two-handed tag on his back just as he was cutting back to the inside. But instead of stopping, he kept running at full speed, and when he crossed the goal line he started jumping up and down and waving the football about over his head. His teammates, who actually weren't in position to see the tag clearly, were running up to congratulate him. Marty, appearing puzzled, drew alongside of me.

"Looked to me like you got him."

"Yeah I got him. When don't I get him? . . . I guess nobody else saw it. He knows I tagged him."

"Maybe he didn't feel it."

"He felt it. He's just trying to get away with something."

"No way" Marty vowed, and he ran up ahead shouting, "Raymond got him. Raymond got him back there. Come back and play it from back here. He was tagged."

"Get out of here" screamed Jerry. "I got a touchdown."

"No you didn't. Raymond tagged you back here."

"He did not!"

"Did so!"

"Oh get the hell outa here. He did not."

"I did so" I shouted back, drawing closer. "You know I tagged you. You're just trying to be some kind of hotshot, that's all."

"Ah you get lost too, Raymond."

"No! You don't tell me to get lost."

"I can tell you all I want. You're just mad I beat you for the touchdown."

"You didn't beat me for any touchdown."

"I did so! I beat you!"

"You did not. If I didn't tag you, then why did I stop running?"

"You just couldn't catch me."

"Aw come on. You know I can beat you by a mile."

"You can not!"

"Can so Jerry. I'll race you right now and prove it."

"That has nothing to do with this. I got a touchdown."

"But I tagged you."

"You did not! I didn't feel any tag. Did anybody see him tag me?" A couple of players from both sides ventured that it looked like I might have tagged him. No one was definite, however, except Marty.

"I saw him tag you. It was clear to me."

"Ah go to hell Marty. You're just brainwashed."

"I am not."

"You are so. Look, I got the touchdown already so let's get the game moving."

"We'll get it moving" I interjected, "as soon as we bring the ball back to where it belongs."

"But it belongs up here! I got a touchdown!" He was so frantically persistent I began wondering if he was sincere about not feeling the tag. But then I dismissed the thought. I mean I just knew the tag had been firm enough. However, in the face of his steadfastedness I was willing to settle for a traditional schoolyard compromise: choosing for it. It was a suggestion thoroughly acceptable to everyone except Jerry.

"No way! I got a touchdown!"

"You did not. I tagged you. I'm giving you a chance to choose for it. Or we can even do the whole play over again. One or the other. But you just can't take a touchdown like that."

"And you just can't take one away either."

"Well let's choose then. You know how they say, cheating shows, never goes."

"Why don't you choose him?" Michael asked. "We're wasting time."

"No! I won't choose him. I got a touchdown!" He became even more worked up, teeth clenched, head shaking vehemently, sandy hair flopping about. I was thinking about conceding the touchdown and then embarassing him with my skill throughout the remainder of the game. I was thinking about this real hard until he said, "You're just a filthy cheatin nigger, that's all. Just a cheatin nigger and that's all you know how to do."

Well my head just exploded inside as the world around me came to a complete standstill. After a moment I could hear my thoughts real good. *Nigger? Me? Now Jerry Weissman got more sense than that. Well ain't he? I knows he don' think he that bad. Do he? Just because he a little bigger than me now, so what.* My palms turned clammy and I cocked my right hand to bust him straight in the mouth. He reeled backwards and I bloodied his nose with another right and followed that with a jump-kick to his stomach. He fell to the ground and I pounced on him and straddled his chest. I yanked him by the collar and peered down into his trembling blue eyes.

"I wish I had a knife" I declared without waver. "I'd stab you straight through the top of your head and kill you. You hear me?" I could tell he believed me. Momentarily, I believed myself. I started shaking him with all of my might. He surged to resist, but he couldn't get loose from my grasp until I finally let him.

Jerry scrambled to his feet. Tears streamed down his cheeks, tears ran into smeared blood. He scooped up the football, you just know it had to be his, and he broke out running. As he passed Marty, Marty punched him on the side of the face with a pretty good left hand. Surprised me by how well he threw it, how coordinated. Jerry staggered forward and I rushed up to boot him in the rear to get him going full tilt again. He hollered back over his shoulder, "I'll get both of you. You wait and see, you filthy cheaters."

The crowd dispersed uneasily and I walked out of the schoolyard behind Marty. He was genuinely as upset as I was.

"Wonder what he's got up his sleeve, Raymond."

"Better be nothing. Best thing for him to do is leave us on alone. I'm not even worried about it."

Jerry apologized the very next day. He still insisted he was right about the game, but admitted he was way out of bounds with the name-calling. He said his own parents told him that he was wrong. I shook hands with him and forgave him verbally — but not inside.

Lonnie Blair was amused by the incident. He couldn't stop laughing and rolling all over his bedroom floor.

"You sure showed that Jewboy somethin, didn't you?"

"Yeah man. I rocked his chops pretty good. Shook his mind up too."

"You did the right thing. Just because you nice enough to play football with them don't give them Jewboys no right to think they can jig over you. That's just like a Jew too, you know, tryin ta take advantage of somebody. You know I'd like to crack me a few of them Jewboys myself. I'm surprised they didn't all jump you. They're good for somethin like that."

"Well I know they probably wanted to, but I was ready for em. I woulda grabbed somebody and choked him until they all backed off. That's the way you do that you know."

"I know."

I didn't tell Lonnie about the loyalty of Marty Rosenberger, or even about how much a friend Marty always was. Lonnie would never have understood.

III

I knew a little all-purpose chemistry by the end of the fifth grade, knew that lack of mortgage payments was a sure-fire formula for foreclosure and eviction. And as a result of this uncompromising bit of science (brought about by slow horses and fast women again), we moved into an apartment about a half mile deeper into Corona, into the heart of what many were calling a two-story slum. Couldn't even get a glimpse of Jackson Heights. Northern Boulevard, as it cut through our neighborhood one block to the south, looked a lot like that old Eighth Avenue. As a matter of fact our neighborhood was often dubbed "Little Harlem."

Old adjustable me tried to fit right in. On my block there was a bunch of Lonnie Blairs to befriend. Of course I would reveal to this group only those parts of me I felt they could best understand, as they did in turn, as we cemented our bonds.

"I'm gon be a major leaguer."

"Aw man Junior, you ain gon be no goddamn major leaguer. Yo fat ass too slow, man. You knock a ball all the way off the center field fence and the man still got time to chase the ball down, stop once or twice to pee, and still throw you out at first base."

"I ain't that damn slow, P.J."

"Aw nigguh, you slower than that. I'll dust you man. I'll give you half a block on a two block race and still dust you. We can go now. I'll show you how slow yo fat ass is."

"Naw man. You got it."

"Yeah I know. I'll pass yo ass so fast you'll think you goin backwards."

"So what man. At least I can hit. Now tell me I can't hit."

"Hell yeah you can hit. Everybody know you goddamn sure can hit. But so what? I can learn to hit like that too. But yo chubby ass ain never gon move no faster. So if any major leaguer gon come outa this here block, it's gotta be me. Ain't that right Robbie Bo?"

"I don't know about that P.J. Maybe Keith can be one too. I mean he good as hell with that glove and handles the rest of the game none too bad."

"Well maybe he'll come after me. I don't care. As long as I'm the first famous nigguh off this block. All right Keith?"

"Don't make me no difference."

"I'll come see yall in every city yall play in" declared Butchie. "I'll be a big time gangster or somethin by then and have mucho money."

"Aw man, you scared to be a gangster."

"What you mean Wallace? I ain't scared."

"Would you kill somebody?"

"Damn right I would. I'll Al Capone a nigguh in a minute. Half a minute if it's a White boy."

While it was mandatory to hate the Whites, we couldn't stand being called Black. That was an automatic fight. Most other jibes were tolerated if done in customary taste, or if the target of the insult was in a decent mood. But, of course, you could never count on either.

"Hey Butchie, yo momma wear combat boots." (An old standard lead.)

"So yo momma don't wear nothin. Most bitches don't when they out hoin' all over town." (Definitely a nonstandard reply.)

Time out for Butchie and P.J.

"Hey Keith, where yo Pops at man?" (Usually fair game.)

"He in his skin nigguh. Where you think he at?" (Not in the mood.)

"Mine's home with me every night dummy." (Pushing the issue.)

"Man, you don't know if that's your real father or not." (Last chance to back off.)

"What the hell you mean I don't?" (Dare you.)

"You know how they say, Wallace. Momma's baby. Daddy's maybe." (Ready.)

"So what you sayin?" (Stall.)

"That there's one more triflin bitch in this world than you thought there was." (Stop stalling.)

Time out for Wallace Jones and Keith Gilyard.

I tried to stay up on my current events and was rewarded by having my senses brutalized by the outrageous happenings in the South. Events like the Meredith affair were occurring steadily. Although it was less than a year since I had been relatively detached concerning Meredith's suffering, I was, nevertheless, quite indignant at the latest outbreaks of bigotry. Negroes were doing simple things like registering to vote and were being greeted by bombs and bullets and cattle prods and rubber hoses and police dogs. Emblazoning my memory. I couldn't believe that the response of most of those Negroes was to continue marching and demonstrating and trying to register. My youthly instinct and vision required that a full-scale war be conducted in the South, not merely a one-sided blitz. I mean if you get hit you got to hit back, right? It seemed simple enough to me. Hell, I felt those Negroes down South didn't have to worry about Krushchev and the Russians. Those Negroes were going to be wiped out by the Ku Klux Klan before then.

For an adult view of the situation I had to go down to the barbershop. Boone told me the issue wasn't as clear cut as it seemed. Mr. Horton, who had grown up in the South, told me I was really too young to worry about vengeance. When I ran into Mr. Shortside, who also had grown up in the South, he told me that the Negroes down there were plum loco if they didn't have better sense than to offer to line up to get billy-clubbed. Shorty was my man. But I knew that Boone and Horton were no fools. And certainly Martin Luther King Jr. was not. I mean he spoke so well. I began to form the uneasy impression that there was something about this whole problem that I wasn't quite grasping yet.

So I was a puzzled spectator that summer. I was immensely proud as I saw more than 250,000 people jam the streets of the nation's capital during the March on Washington. Felt proud as I listened to Martin's speech of ideal integration. I knew Martin had a beautiful dream. And with all those people rallying around the Lincoln Monument, on televi-

sion they seemed like damn near all the folks in the world, I thought there
was enough strength available to make King's dream come to life. Wasn't
any way that glorious day was supposed to be followed by the bombing
of a Negro church in Birmingham, Alabama. Four more Black casualties.
Young girls. Like Sherry and Judy and Debra Lynn.

"Hey Keith, my grandma lives down there in Alabama."

"That ain't nothin Robbie Bo. Mine's too."

"Yeah? Well they better not start no stuff like that in my grandma's
town."

"They better not do it in my grandma's town neither."

"And you know these honkies up here better not start no stuff like
that. We'd really have to take care of them then."

"You right Robbie Bo. We'd have to."

My biggest hero that summer was Sherry. She was on her way to
junior high school in the fall and a place in a Special Progress class, the
only Black I knew who had made one. She didn't make it from the one
class; she had been in 6-2, which should have tipped me off, but her marks
on all the standardized exams were so high that she was included anyway.
Now she had a chance to do the seventh and eighth grades in one year.
That two-year program was rough. The three-year program was enriched,
but you didn't skip any time. It was more prestige than pressure.

I was permitted to remain at 149 for my final year of elementary
school and I started the term with great zeal. Naturally. I couldn't wait
to make S.P. myself. Fortunately I was up to the task because 6-1 was the
most competitive class I had ever been in. Whenever I went up to Mrs.
Kessler's desk to pick up a test, I was mugged by someone anxious to see
what grade I had received. Everyone in the class had the news before I
even reached my seat. Our 100s were waved about jubilantly like flags
and our 70s somehow managed to get lost. I had my share of flags and
wasn't worried.

Sherry asked out of S.P. after only one marking period. It had been too
much cramming for her, too much emphasis on fierce competition. She was
too introverted to handle the pressure cooker. They couldn't take away her
intelligence, but they couldn't make her knock heads either. She really
wanted no part of special progress at all. Not in a one class or an S.P. class.
She was transferred to one of the average classes and she flourished.

I wasn't too disappointed in Sherry. Even then I could understand that
she had been more victim than failure. I just wished I could have lent her
my guile, spirit, and ability to hang tough.

Judy and Debra Lynn, who was beginning kindergarten, were over
at 92, the midget reformatory. I just hoped they didn't have to fight.

The Negro got himself into further trouble, if you can imagine that, when Kennedy was assassinated. At least that's what some of the older folks in the neighborhood were saying. Said he was the Negro's best friend and that the Negro would be at a great disadvantage without him around. I had nothing personal against Kennedy, but I didn't think he and the Negro were ever quite like Lonnie Blair and me. Lonnie would never watch anybody harm me.

What shook me the most that year was the controversy that stemmed from the announcement by the Board of Education that a plan was under consideration to "pair" 92 and 149 in order to desegregate both facilities. Like most residents of Corona, I was in favor of the idea. Of course I would be out of elementary school by the time the plan was implemented, but I thought the plan would make school better for Judy and Debra Lynn, give them a better opportunity to learn. And these two schools were so close together that busing wasn't even part of the issue.

Regardless, most of the people in Jackson Heights were dead set against the plan. There were numerous threats and lawsuits on their behalf. A series of articles was run in the *New York Times* exploring this and other aspects of Northern White Prejudice. Boone saved the paper for me each day and I devoured the accounts. Paid particular attention to how White folks, while allowing themselves to be quoted only anonymously, were trying to justify their ways of thinking. Lame reasoning such as:

> I feel that every group should have their equal rights. But I look at this thing as the other side trying to obtain their equal rights by taking over mine. . . .

and

> I wish there was some way for everything to be integrated peacefully — you know, there could be one or two colored at first and maybe more later, and nobody would mind — I know that nobody would mind. It's just the large number that I'm afraid of. And that's what everybody else is afraid of too. Not just in housing, but in the schools, too. . . .

and

> Look, it's not just me. Everybody does this. You tell your friend that there are plenty of places he can find an apartment, across Junction Boulevard. . . .

and

> The educated get along pretty well. At the United Nations they sit and talk together all day, and talk together all night, and they eat dinner together and go to each other's houses, and they get along. But the lower classes never can get along. They'll always be fighting with each other. Now, right now, the colored is in the lower class. . . .

Langston Hughes and Mr. Shortside had always contended that a thick vein of prejudice was all around us up here, and I had come to believe them. But now I had it all in print. Positive proof straight from Whitey's own mouth. And what unsettled me so much was that I began wondering if I actually knew any of the people quoted in the newspapers. Had I been in any of their homes? Had I played with their children? Did Michael Stein's mother really hate me and only pretend to be fond of me?

It became easier to forego the usual activities in the playground and either join Lonnie in Junction Park or take an early hike up to the block. When I did play with my classmates I didn't coast any more. Played hard.

I wrote a stinging attack on White Backlash that brought acclaim from my classmates, teacher, principal, and other schoolmates. I basically argued that the only way to correct injustice is all at once. Anything short of that is but more injustice. The logic was simple. And in addition to my general argument, with the *Times* as my evidence, I made reference to what was happening right in Jackson Heights.

The essay stayed on the bulletin board through two "marquee" changes. Of course I doubted the sincerity of all the approval I received, all except that of my Black schoolmates. They were the only ones in that environment who possessed a fervently expressed indignation to match mine over the nerve of some White folks to demonstrate or insinuate by word or deed that Blacks wanted too much too soon.

Lonnie Blair, unlike Mrs. Kessler and Mr. Price, knew what restraint went into that piece of writing. Lonnie knew I had really just highlighted the basic issues, hadn't told them about all the stuff we had been hearing from this new guy named Malcolm.

The term dragged to its final day and I wound up with a long string of "excellents" on my report card, bagged that S.P. spot easily. I wouldn't be going to junior high school in Jackson Heights with the others. I was out of the zone. The fact that my own sister was already enrolled in the school didn't seem to make any difference to anyone in charge. She could remain, but I wasn't welcome. Michael wondered if I would ever come to see him. I said I probably would.

That same afternoon we had a softball game going in the park. I had just hustled into third base with a triple when I happened to look up and see Lonnie Blair, along with a group of his friends from 92, climbing through the hole in the right field fence. As they all bopped in from the outfield I knew trouble was coming.

James Bishop, a sturdy kid, started hassling Leonard Landau in the batter's box. "Lemme git a hit."

"But we're playing a game. You're not supposed to interrupt a game just like that."

"Aw gimme the bat you White asshole. I know what I'm suppose to do." James snatched the bat away, shoved Leonard aside, and assumed a batting stance. "Come on Blondie" he called out to the pitcher, Mark Greenberg. "Come on and throw the ball."

Mark held the ball in his glove and didn't say anything. This was the opening James was looking for.

"Oh, so you think you bad, hunh?" He dropped the bat and headed slowly toward the mound. By this time Lonnie was standing at third base with me. His presence had caused Barry Weinstein, the third baseman, to ease over next to Barry Goldberg at shortstop.

"That boy gon git his ass beat now" Lonnie said matter of factly.

"He shoulda thrown the ball" I replied.

"Yeah, maybe so. But somebody gotta git their ass beat down here. Maybe everybody. 'Cept you know ain nobody gon mess with you."

"I know ain't nobody messin with me. It's these gray boys that's in trouble and I don't care nothin bout that. I'll even git down myself if you want me to."

"Nah Keith, you don't hafta do that. We don't need no extra help for this, probably won't bust them up that much anyhow. All depends on how bad they jump. I'm just gon try to git somebody to hit me first or call me a nigger or somethin so I can stomp him. Won't nobody be able to blame me neither. School's over now."

"Yeah Lonnie" I said, slapping him five and grinning. "School's really over now."

James kept pushing Mark around pretty hard but wouldn't tee off and really nail him. Like Lonnie, he was waiting to be offended. But Mark simply kept collecting himself long enough to ask "Why don't you stop it?" before getting pushed all over again. The spectators were laughing and the ballplayers were terrified. All except Marty Rosenberger. I saw his face redden as he sat on the edge of the dugout bench next to John Levy. I could picture him running out to take up for Mark Greenberg and getting thoroughly thrashed, a classic case of will without skill. Even as I stood with Lonnie Blair beside me, I knew that I could not allow Marty to get hurt.

Mark got pushed again, and he looked over at me as if he thought I could do a little negotiating. I became aware that most of the other ballplayers were casting glances at me also, wishing I could be their champion, their general. They had to be crazy. Number one, I didn't want to bail them out. Number two, it wasn't possible anyway.

James shoved Mark to the ground and headed over toward the short-stop position. The other Black kids fanned out to enact their own scenes of harassment, of baiting.

Lonnie Blair focused on the dugout. "Guess I'll jig with somebody in there."

"Me too Lonnie."

"Nah man, you don't have to."

"But I want to. These gray boys been gittin on my nerves too much anyway." I ran over ahead of Lonnie, ferociously shoved Marty Rosenberger to the ground and pinned him there by sitting on his chest, using the dugout fence to brace myself.

"Hey get off me" Marty protested. "What the hell do you think you're doing?"

"Shut up you little Jewish punk bitch before I get up and stomp your ass."

John Levy was horrified by my words, but Lonnie Blair roared approvingly. Then he grabbed John's bat and began swinging it wildly (though really with control as he was careful not to hit John). But John, unable to read the action correctly, fled the dugout in panic, his perceived attacker right on his heels.

"Get off of me Raymond" Marty balked. "What the hell are you pulling?" He struggled to get loose but I easily held my position.

"Take it easy" I whispered. "I'm trying to keep you from getting hurt. I know you Marty. You'll get out there running your mouth and get yourself hurt."

"But look Raymond, I'm not scared." Now his whisper equalled mine.

"I know you're not scared, but everybody else is."

"That's their problem."

"No it's your problem because you'll be the one on the spot. Believe me. I know what I'm talking about."

"But those guys are just bullying people. It's not fair."

"But it's fair what I'm doing. And if you don't think so then maybe we can get up and fight for real. I'll kick your ass myself. I'll be just like them."

"But I know you're not."

"Look Marty, you don't know anything. So just relax and shut up."

Marty only put up a token struggle after that and from our peculiar entanglement we saw the action draw to a close. We saw that no one put up enough resistance to get roughed up very much, and we saw James snatch the gloves of both Barrys and sprint away. A couple of his partners took gloves also, and then all of them began to speed away. Lonnie held up his new bat like a torch and followed, calling back over his shoulder, "Hey Keith we gotta split man. Come on."

"Yeah man. Hold up." I hopped up, offered Marty a weak "Take care" and dashed out toward right field, past the blurred white faces, running straight for that hole in the fence.

There would be no coming back in the years to come. I never knew how Marty eventually explained me to the boys in the past. I never knew how this final scene of this six-year drama affected them as a group.

My fellows up ahead, well, they had hate on their backs but not really in their hearts. They had a lot of toughening up to do.

As for me, oh the deep me, if I could just reach high and far. . . .

IV

Summer 1964. President Johnson pushed another Civil Rights Act through Congress. It was supposedly a guarantee for the desegregation of public facilities as well as an assurance that a policy of affirmative action would be widely implemented. What it actually was, in the esteemed opinion of Mr. Shortside, was just another piece of toilet tissue legislation.

A White cop in Harlem shot a fifteen-year-old Black boy, an event that set off a series of riots up in the old home town. Johnson speculated that communist forces had instigated the riots and he sent in the FBI to investigate.

It was "Freedom Summer" in the South. The key object was to increase the registration of Negro voters. But the Klansmen kicked off the drive by murdering Chaney, Goodman, and Schwerner and dramatically reaffirming that they would just as soon kill a White sympathizer, especially a Jew, as kill a Negro himself. Boone said he had seen it coming.

I suggested to Mr. Horton that maybe Johnson should evacuate everyone from Mississippi except the Klan and then drop the atom bomb on Mississippi just as Truman dropped it on Hiroshima. Mr. Horton suggested once again that I could get a little too serious-minded at times.

Perhaps Mr. Horton had a point. After all, I was almost a teenager. Wasn't it time to stop worrying about these weighty matters? I mean the outline of my life was fairly clear. All I had to do was protect my own self, finish growing up, and grab my piece of the glory. Relax as much as possible for now, you know, cool out with my friends and enjoy my surroundings. Stop worrying about such great conquests. Spend the summer being as much kid as I could be. And the main battle a kid had in the summer was to beat the heat.

The World's Fair was a major outlet, and I considered it the greatest exposition ever created. Coney Island or the circus or the Museum of Natural History didn't even come close. We residents of Corona were the luckiest of people because the fairgrounds were like a local park for us. Visitors were streaming in by the thousands from all over the world to reach the same place we could reach with a twenty-minute walk. We had the most time to see everything the fair had to offer, from the Unisphere to the Watusi dancers in loin cloths and Converse sneakers. We had more chances than anyone else to run around all the pavilions and witness just how diverse and brilliant humans could be.

We were elated at how the whiz kids at General Motors, Chrysler, and American Telephone and Telegraph were going to make the future such an easy and convenient place in which to live. As resourceful as they were, they had us believing we would all own a telephone with a video screen and a flying car like George Jetson by the time we were thirty. I thought the folks at National Cash Register were superbly ingenious as they had developed a transparent slide, which wasn't much bigger than a book of matches, on which the entire *Bible* was reproduced. And I must have watched the display of nuclear fusion in the General Electric Pavilion at least fifty times. It was a fresh thrill each time they heated the chamber of deuterium to forty million degrees to produce that thunder and lightning effect in the exhibit hall. It was as if I, myself, had made a discovery. And you know I had to check out the rockets, those magnificent missiles. They had one rocket so massive they couldn't even assemble the whole thing for display and that, naturally, made it seem all the more awesome. Only thing that spoiled the attraction was that it kept me wondering about what the Soviet Union had. But the Russians, of course, weren't represented.

So we roamed the fair at will, the nappy-headed boys of curiosity. First we'd see the exhibits that were free and then we'd sneak or beg or pay our way into the others. We put in a good share of our time on the rides, mostly the monorail and the Pepsi Cola Tour of the Globe. We came to know the fair so well that by the time our parents got around to taking us we were qualified to give them a guided tour. Most of us didn't actively assume the guide role though; we let our parents think they were introducing us to the fun.

One morning Wallace Jones and I had romped about the fairgrounds so much that our feet were sore. We were hungry also since our money had been on the low side that day, and that made us especially anxious to head for home. Gingerly we stepped out onto Roosevelt Avenue beneath the El train roaring by overhead. They had all new cars on the line for the fair. I watched sparks jump from the rails. Wallace pointed across the road to deserted Shea Stadium.

"Look Keith, the Mets act like they never wanna come back home. What the hell is wrong with them?"

"Ain't nothin wrong. That's just the way the schedule runnin. They'll be back next week. Milwaukee Braves comin in too."

"Good. I been waitin to check out Hank Aaron. I wish they was over there now so we could sneak on in."

"I don't know Wallace. I'm so tired all I wanna do is git home. But after I rest up I'm goin hustlin. You still goin, right?"

I couldn't get an answer just then. Wallace had spotted two White boys pedaling our way, heading toward Flushing. You could often catch White boys cycling down Roosevelt that way, skirting along the back edge of dark town. As they drew close we could see that they were about our own age. Maybe one was a year or two younger. Both sported a carrot top, a freckled face, and a set of big ears. Unmistakably brothers.

"Let's scare em up" Wallace suggested.

"I'm down" I promptly responded.

Wallace rushed out into the street to become a human road block, and before I joined him I sucked in a good long breath to summon vitality back into my frame. I was stretching past five feet by then, like Wallace, with almost ninety pounds to push somebody around with.

The older boy reacted first. He tried to steer his sleek ten speed wide of Wallace, but he wasn't lucky enough to catch any traffic coming to run interference for him and Wallace ran him down easily. Pinned him in against the opposite curb. The younger brother panicked and almost fell from his gold-colored ten speed. When I grabbed hold of his handle bars I actually steadied his bike and prevented him from toppling over.

"Hey what's wrong with you?" he squealed.

"Ain't nothin wrong with me, stupid. What's wrong with you? That's what you should be tryin to figure out. You're the one with the problem."

"I don't have any problem."

"Don't think so hunh? Well maybe you can figure it out next time you look in the mirror. It ain't Howdy Doody Time out here you know, you little freckle-faced punk."

He looked fretfully over to the other side of the road and my eyes followed him, just in time to see Wallace haul off and punch this other poor guy right upside the head. The carrot top was no timid fellow though; he took a clumsy swipe at my friend but missed as Wallace danced back out of range. The boy was more than willing to tangle, however, and he climbed off of his bike to mix it up. They exchanged a few quick and solid blows, but then Wallace got shrewd and delivered a powerful kick to the groin. It was a favorite maneuver from a type of kick boxing we referred to as Stato, and Wallace had definitely statoed his opponent good. The boy slumped to the ground and Wallace ran around him to grab his bike.

My own carrot top became hysterical and left me holding his bicycle as he hopped off and dashed wildly toward his fallen brother. And just then a beat-in green Chevy screeched and slanted in toward Wallace. A stout man with long black hair and a taped-up stick scrambled from the car to give chase. He was waving his weapon and yelling menacingly, "Hey you fucking black nigger. Get your ass back here. I'll break your fucking nigger neck if I catch you, you black nigger you."

The man was surprisingly fast, but not nearly fast enough to catch the speeding Wallace Jones, who was pedaling furiously. The man hurled his club viciously, aimed it straight at the back of Wallace's head. As it fell wide of the mark he cried out in anguish. "I'd like to break your freaking ass for you, you lousy black dog."

As I watched this man perform it became immediately obvious to me what I had to do, so I mounted that shiny gold-colored ten speed and took off in the opposite direction just as swiftly as I could. My first major theft. And I didn't even have to give it much thought.

My fear was barely under control as I started a careful but speedy zig-zag pattern, turning at every corner, ever watchful for the wrathful samaritan propelling the green Chevrolet. I told myself I was angry at Wallace for forcing my hand, but I was unconvincing, and with each ensuing pedal the realization grew within me that I would gladly have volunteered had I known this adventure would feel so great. It was a sensation that outweighed any sense of guilt and, predictably, I was quick to rationalize.

Sure I had a bicycle at home, a decent second-hand three speed. But it was broken now, a problem with the back sprocket, and a new back wheel would cost more than the whole bike did. Forget it. I deserved a nice shiny ten speed and figured the White boy could get a replacement far faster than I would have been given an original. So this was like a Robin Hood thing. Besides, didn't I have to take this bicycle or get killed by a maniac?

The bicycle caper made us heroes on the block. Big Rob (who used to be Robbie Bo) was immensely pleased. He was fourteen now, involved with street gangs, and suddenly too old to hang around with us. But he still served as a role model and commended us for having heart. Other guys more our age were quite willing to have heart also, and a bike stealing boom was set off.

We doubled up on the bikes we already had and went scouting out in White neighborhoods. When we spotted a prospect we dropped off one of the piggyback riders. He knew that if he backed out he would be stranded, so he always snipped the chain, raided the yard, threw the punch, or did whatever else was necessary. In brief order we each had a handsome ten speed. Then we argued about who had the handsomest and began stealing all over again. Sometimes we simply traded in a good bike for a better one, you know, left the victim something to get by okay.

The backyard of Wallace and P.J. became our workshop. Their father didn't pay us much attention, and we were constantly filing off serial numbers, painting frames, and switching parts. Whenever we surfaced on one of our creations we'd tell our parents we had borrowed a bike from a friend. It was a rather thin line but they didn't question it much. And the bikes kept rolling in. We found allies on surrounding blocks and things eventually reached the point where stolen bike reports were flooding the 109th, the 110th, and the 114th precincts. The *Long Island Press* even ran a story about a suspected organized bike ring in the area. We all had to laugh about that one. We had been organized largely by impetuosity, and our only real profit was our own excitement.

Every now and then, however, we had to let the bicycles rest. Wallace was almost caught by the police before he could make it back to the workshop. The squad car, with the little White boy in the back seat, circled the block about six times before we were left alone. But we knew they were too suspicious. Time to cool out for a spell. Little matter, there were other activities that had to be squeezed into our days and we didn't have to be pedaling to do them.

We had to keep trying our hand at sports, although maybe not with the best of sportsmanship. I mean we had a baseball team that would have scared the Bad News Bears off the field. And we had to jog the few blocks on down to Flushing Bay. Didn't care if the tide was out; the resulting stench never bothered us all that much. The usual challenges down there were to see who could be the ones to catch the first polluted eel, stone a rat to death, or skip a pebble across the water better than anyone else.

Sometimes we would just sit on the benches and watch the airplanes take off and land at LaGuardia, which was at the western end of the bay. For some reason, one of us invariably wanted to fly to Mexico. A more reachable fantasy was found down toward the eastern end of the bay, at the marina, where we could actually sneak on the boats that were anchored there. We couldn't figure out a way to sail anywhere, but despite that small inconvenience the marina was one of the greatest locations for dreaming.

We each usually picked our own private boat to relax in. The tan and olive *Betsy's Delight* was my personal favorite, and I figured I wouldn't mind meeting Betsy herself one day. Our tastes were so similar. But alas, I covered my tracks so well I was positive that Betsy didn't even know I existed. In fact, we all had the utmost respect for our boats; I mean they had such a soothing effect on us. We would bring hooks and sinkers and strings, and fish lazily for eels that we usually tossed back into the water. Or maybe find a mellow station on our portable radios and watch the sun droop to the tune of "Girl from Ipanema." Or maybe just lie back and close our eyes and listen to the waves ripple and dash up against the sides of our floating paradises.

One evening we went to the marina to find that an unconquerable barbed wire fence had been erected to keep us out. We later learned that this action had been taken because a group of vandals had used our boats for graffiti practice. So that canceled out our evenings of tranquility at the bay, but at least we still had lover's lane. We generally saw a pretty decent show of foreplay before being chased, so we didn't much mind being run off from the cars, but we would have paid anything to see what was going on inside those Volkswagen vans that were popular that summer. And it was near where they had been parked that we often found used prophylactics, which one of us would manage to nudge onto the edge of a stick and chase everyone with. I ran some of my fastest sprints to avoid getting tagged by a used rubber.

We were acquiring all types of sexual knowledge and naturally we had to share as much of it as possible with the girls, or was it the other way around? Whatever. The boys with skinned knees had become afflicted with that biggest of curiosities, and the girls, with their hair flying everywhich-a-way, had bodies that promised to charm up more trouble than they were prepared to handle. We spent hours playing Spin the Bottle or indulging in a stimulting little game known as Truth? Dare? Consequences? Promise? or Repeat? We should have just called the game "Dare" because that's the only option anyone ever selected, and that's how most of us obtained our first passionate caresses and long soulful tongue kisses, in other words, that's how we first "macked out." White folks "made out," so I guess we had no choice but to call what we did something different. And there was an all-the-way dare, but I never saw it accepted in public. A lot of behind-the-scenes daring was also going on, however, and when discussing this activity it was difficult, as you would imagine, to distinguish fact from fantasy.

And there were still other things to squeeze in. The price of many of our favorite sodas jumped from thirteen cents to fifteen cents down at Mr. Jordan's that summer and we couldn't appreciate it at all, so we formed a syndicate to protest, or rather, to threaten. We cut print from the newspaper (so detectives couldn't trace our handwriting, a Dick Tracy idea) and we composed a message to slip under Mr. Jordan's door warning him to roll back prices or else. Of course Mr. Jordan chose to settle for the "else" and we proceeded to sneak out far more things in our clothes than we ever paid for. We probably wanted to do it anyway. But since he was a feeble old Black man I guess we needed that sense of justification. I know it helped me a lot. And about the only time we gave Mr. Jordan a break was when one of the delivery trucks came around. Then we concentrated on raiding the truck.

Now we were so close to home that those truck raids were something we shouldn't have been able to carry out regularly without someone informing our parents. But as I look back I realize our success was due largely to the disintegration of an important community concept. The old practice of "he's a child of the neighborhood so I'll straighten him out first and then take him home to get straightened out some more" had virtually faded out. The code of "we had better mind our business" was prevalent. And we took full advantage.

Even more things to squeeze in. Watching Yogi take a fling as manager. Watching the Phillies blow the best chance they ever had. Winning a marbles championship, becoming superior at jacks, trying to make a spinning top spin for an eternity. Building a go-cart for the races, taking a shot at raising pigeons. A skateboard, a pair of skates, a yo-yo, a unicycle, a bo-lo paddle, boxing gloves, a limbo stick, a jump rope (just to be near the girls). And always moving to the music, always being the music. We had to dance all over the street, just as the record said, and there were so many steps to learn.

7
The Self, Advancing Literacy, and Sidewalk University

Purkey (1970) describes the self as a "complex and dynamic system of beliefs which an individual holds true about himself, each with a corresponding value" (p. 7). With this concept in mind, I will reflect in this chapter on the self that emerged in "Big Fame." Of primary concern is the manner in which my linguistic abilities grew relative to this network of constructs. Naturally, since I view discussions of the self and linguistic growth as woefully incomplete without some attention to aspects of the social transactions affecting both, such perspective, as was the case in earlier chapters, will be provided. Furthermore, I will examine selected experiences of other children.

A belief I held very dearly throughout the elementary school years, one that reverberates throughout the narrative, is that I was destined to become someone important in mainstream society. As a consequence I also placed a high value on possessing a well-developed set of language skills. Such skills were a synonym for the academic progress in school that I believed would secure my inevitable recognition. My advancing language skills, in turn, because they were a measure of how well I could do in my "training ground," served to further solidify my belief in my eventual prominence. My proficiency in language use, therefore, was inextricably bound up with my emerging self. Or as Britton (1982) puts it, "we master language by using it to make the most of our lives" (p. 205).

An Advanced Literacy Set

At the close of my elementary school career I was rated excellent in reading, written communication, spelling, handwriting, and oral communication (see Table 3 in Appendix). I had earned admittance to a special progress class. In the Outstanding Abilities section of the Guidance Data column, I was described as "an eloquent speaker and very much interested in social studies." I was also judged to be a fine athlete. Moreover, my performance in school had previously solicited the remark from my fifth-grade teacher that "poetry-creative writing" was my outstanding interest. Also, not coincidentally, in grades five and six I was recognized by my teachers, for the first time since I left Harlem, as a good leader. All these evaluations are consonant with information given in "Big Fame." However, what may not be so apparent is how directly related these comments are to the specific manner in which I constructed my advanced literacy set (to expand on Holdaway's term). I will endeavor to make the connection clearer.

During the latter half of elementary school my writing ability came to the fore; at least that is how my memory informs me. As mentioned in earlier portions of the narrative, I have some vague notion of earlier writing activities such as handwriting drills, spelling tests, compositions, and book reports. But aside from that, there are no memories from the period prior to fourth grade comparable to the sharp recall expressed earlier about my initial reading experiences. In fact, when I began the essay portions of this book, I was somewhat alarmed that no such recollections were evidenced in the narrative. Unable to imagine that the one ability around which the whole project most revolved should receive such little mention, I viewed the lack of anecdotes about writing development as a flaw. However, I came to realize there would be no reason for my earliest attempts at writing to stand out since they were not accompanied by any difficulty or trauma (such as the bloodshed that underscored my initial tries at reading). Only a writing event of great magnitude, which I viewed my venture into poetry writing to be, would leave the indelible impression later capturable in autobiography.

Another way of framing this is to say that writing only appeared significant to me when I could use it as a means of expressing myself. My experience was similar to what Bissex observed. "The development of writing . . . was part of the development of the person rather than the product of an instructional skills sequence" (p. 108). In my case, writing development was so little a part of a skills sequence that I even curtailed my participation in such instruction. As revealed in the text, the most severe reprimand I received from my teacher in the fourth grade was for not keeping my language arts workbook up to date. It didn't seem to matter to her that my writing ability was up to date. The teacher, in fact, was caught up in contradiction, for in encouraging my creativity by exposing me to more and more poetry, she effectively helped to stifle my patience with workbooks, especially since doing fill-ins neither aided my expressive ability nor taught me anything new about grammar. The last reality was made ostensible by the fact I could run through an entire workbook in one day. So despite her chastisement and that of subsequent teachers for not doing language arts homework, the bottom line for me was that I was becoming the poet-essayist I wished to become. This would always get me judged on the personality scale as "evading responsibility"— though I was being totally responsible to my emerging self.

I don't recall much poetry other than "Space Poem." There was a poem about Clupzitzobop that several classmates enjoyed. And besides the essay on White Backlash, which received so much attention, I vaguely remember doing a piece about automation. I wasn't a prolific writer, nor am I now. I treat writing much as I treat old friends. I don't visit as much as I should, but I'll not hesitate to burden it with my greatest problems. In a time of crisis, which essentially means I need to reweave or perhaps just repair or maybe attach a sleeve to the basic fabric of the self, such as how to value impending fatherhood, I can get very busy with a pen.

It is useful to conceive of my writing ability as having been funded by my reading and oral skills. The narrative informs us that my teacher helped to promote my early poetry experiments by urging me to read Nash and Hughes. (Kozol would have been proud of her.) What is not mentioned in the text, but is implied, is that we had been exposed to poetry in class prior to our own attempts to write some. Certainly by then I had read the full offering of books by Dr. Seuss. And as I look back again at "Space Poem" it is clear to me that my rhythmic and rhyming patterns owed much to that exposure. So here is a rather simple case of reading funding writing.

Of course poetry wasn't all I read. There were the science fiction books, the comic books, the child-detective and adventure books, the encyclopedia my mother insisted we have despite its cost. We got her money's worth.

My interest in sports made reading about sports necessary. I collected a large number of sports magazines and established my usually still enforced sports-pages-first policy of reading the daily newspapers. But I did get around to the front sections. As my teacher noted, I was keenly interested in social studies. I had to keep up with the space race and the KKK.

With the reading program I had underway, which was critical in developing that skill itself, my writing was bound to flourish also. This dynamic is described further by Mayher, Lester, and Pradl (1983):

> In all, the written material provides ideas, sources, points of view, and sometimes models for students to use in their own writing. Another, less explicit, benefit is that the more reading our students do, the more possible it is for them to develop an "ear" for the written language.
>
> That's a strange analogy, in one sense, since we're talking about reading, not listening. How *does* reading develop your "ear" for language? We're often confronted with questions about how students learn to write complete sentences; how they learn about organization and coherence; how they learn all these things if they're not directly taught. Much of this is learned through talk, but some of the unique characteristics of the written language can only be learned through reading and writing. By providing students with a wide range of reading material—from poems to editorials to technical reports—we're giving them examples of writing that employ the features we wish them to use. The more they read this material, the better they'll become attuned to acceptable standard written English. (p. 109)

My oral skills were an equally important source of funding for my developing writing. It was largely through conversation that I was able to gauge how the self I expressed in writing was being received by others, thus enabling me to adjust my self-concept in ways I deemed appropriate, in essence, to create the self I would express in subsequent writing.

I was bombarded with so many contradictory stimuli that I had to be a garrulous child in order to organize it all. I was delving into the lives of my classmates, gaining a more highly developed sense of how individuals belonging to other segments of society lived. I was also more deeply concerned with racial discrimination in America and with modifying my stance toward the larger society while keeping a range of community sentiments in mind. I had a lot of mental synthesizing to do, and I decided to do much of it during those large, six-hour chunks of time spent in school. I would sneakily chatter as much as I could but, unlike some of my classmates, I was never afraid to ramble on for the general public. I spoke when called on, actually campaigned to be called on, volunteered to give speeches—and still was a disruptive chatterer.

Perpetual talking was the reason I would never receive an "excellent" in Social Living, though I was apparently socializing very well. After all, I wasn't talking to myself. But I always received a "fair." Even the G given to me at the end of sixth grade (see Table 3 in Appendix) was superimposed over an F, which shows there was maybe some hesitancy over the matter. Again, as with the admonition for lagging behind in the workbook, my teachers didn't realize how the deviance made the normative behavior possible. For I never talked when writing was assigned, though my talk was indeed an important prelude to those occasions. While it cannot be denied that I experienced certain value conflicts that militated against my ever being very "disciplined" in school, and this is especially true in the later years, I suspect, nevertheless, that I would have been less of a "behavior problem" and maybe even a better writer if my teachers had exhibited an understanding similar to that found in the work of Martin et al. (1976):

> We think a school could be, and should be, an environment in which all kinds of talk do — in fact — happen; where children can talk to adults in both formal and informal situations, where purposive, or directed talk goes on — as it always has — and where undirected and unconstrained conversations are also seen as part of the educative process. (p. 17)

There was a strong collective desire to talk informally in those classrooms. As stated earlier, I could always find various partners for conversation. This was true even though none of them as individuals would dare chatter for any lengthy stretch. I had more nerve than the rest of the class, but I can hardly prove I had more need. Who knows what frustration lingered at the base of their relative conformity?

What *I* am most positive of is that because of the ability I possessed in reading, writing, and speaking, much of which developed despite the constricting nature of some aspects of schooling, I departed from elementary school as a confident user of a language accepted in the mainstream. By remaining my own best guardian of the self, I had realized a great deal of the communicative potential I had first brought to school.

The Bent-But-Not-Broken Home

At this point I will address more directly the concept of the "broken home." Along with the eradicationist spiel, this concept has long been used by educators to generate pat explanations for many problems exhibited by African-American students in school. Because the closing section of "Big Fame" shows that I was primed to "act out," it is imperative that the relationship between my home life and school progress receive a bit more discussion.

School records indicate that my outstanding disability was "father not living with family" (see Table 1 in Appendix). It was not enough "disability," however, to keep either me or my sister from going to special progress classes in junior high school. That would have been an observation worth recording, for such remarks would at least have highlighted how much emphasis was put on education in our home. But it's always been especially difficult for teachers to break molds. The most thoughtful (and mold-breaking) comments made by any of mine relative to the issue was the question mark offered by my fifth-grade teacher and the blank spot left by my sixth-grade teacher when asked to evaluate my relationship to my parents (see Table 2 in Appendix). They wouldn't even pretend to understand it.

Nor am I the ultimate authority. But I will state unequivocally that the consistent belief in my ability shown by both of my parents was a major reason I was always, for one thing, in better shape than the school system itself.

Sure there were family difficulties, but the contention that they were directly translated into school problems is ludicrous. To label my "broken home" a learning disability represents, among other things, a failure to view me as an active participant in my own reality and a refusal to see that I had to wrestle with the clash between public school values and the values of the street school, often referred to in the streets as Sidewalk University. The narrative clearly illustrates the conflict, which was the crucial tension I had to deal with, a tension largely produced by knowledge of some of the contradictions inherent in the mainstream world of which I longed to be a part. It wasn't my father who persecuted James Meredith.

The most dramatic impact my father could have had on altering the course of my life after elementary school would have been to keep me out of Sidewalk University. Whether he could have done that is, I think, unlikely; it is definitely unknowable. We do know that I enrolled.

Sidewalk U

The one belief I held above all others, including the one of "destiny," was that I should fit in with my community peers, which meant adopting their value system and, in fact, helping to develop it. Even the hope for success expressed at the close of the schoolyard scene was done in the context of running with the "crew." The contradiction was powerful. Up to that point, due to adroit impression management, I had been able to give convincing performances before both school and street audiences. But it was inevitable that my act before one group would suffer, lending strength to my presentation before the other. In refusing to jeopardize my peer ties in the community, I made a decision well understood by Eugene Perkins (1975):

> If he chooses to withdraw, and few do, then he will find himself being the scapegoat of his community. The exclusion from the dominant culture patterns of the community could also cause him great anxieties and possibly

serious psychological problems. The norm for social deviancy is often different in the black ghetcolony, and sometimes the child who tries to emulate
so-called conventional behavior is seen as being more deviant than one who
openly violates certain conventional standards. (p. 29)

I became very active, and in many ways a leader, in a cultural system
in which taking from Whites was congratulated and a militant political
orientation was favored over the moderate stance the school system, and
the home for that matter, would have me assume. In our group, modera-
tion concerning issues of race relations was defined as backwardness. We
felt that Black political activists should receive all they demanded right
then and there.

Perkins, whose work has been much too underpublicized, offers a tax-
onomy of character types usually found among the youth of the Black
community. Although there is no precise one-to-one correspondence between the traits I possessed and any of the types he presents, my increased
involvement in the Street Institution, as he calls it, can accurately be understood, nonetheless, as my movement from being a "Regular" to becoming
a "Cool Cat."

> The Regular is an accepted member in the Street Institution although he is
> not bound to all of its norms. He is the youngster who gets along with almost
> everyone without compromising his own value system. His ability to interact
> with his peers, and not be totally influenced by them, is a tribute to his
> uniqueness.
>
> He is "one of the boys" and again he is not. The Regular is able to vacil-
> late roles because he has never made a full commitment to the Street Institu-
> tion. Actually his primary values are closer to white middle class values than
> those of his peers. He is usually a good student, conforms to most conven-
> tional laws, has close family ties and rarely belongs to a gang. Yet, despite
> this allegiance to white middle class norms, he knows enough about the
> Street Institution to function within it without undue stress. Because his cop-
> ing posture is more flexible than his peers, he is able to "free enterprise" and
> engage in only those activities which he feels are relatively safe. (pp. 11–12)

As a Regular I could both entertain and withstand my blood brother,
adjust to new surroundings, and keep Shorty's information from directly
fueling drastic behavior. As a Cool Cat, however, I was expected to provide certain guidance for my community peers. Clarity of position was
required concerning fundamental matters such as the plight of Blacks.
And although I didn't have to be flamboyant, which could even be a negative trait, my identification with the group had to be firm. If it hadn't
been, I could not have become a Cool Cat in the first place. Perkins describes my role well:

The Cool Cat is probably the most imitated of the lot. Being cool is very important in the ghetcolony. When things go down in the ghetcolony, such as intense police harassment, it is advantageous to be cool. When situations become "uptight," being cool is a trademark of street sophistication. Black children learn how to be cool under the most extenuating circumstances. Being cool implies that one is "hip," "together," and is able to function under considerable pressure. It becomes a stabilizer that allows one to minimize threatening situations and ignore others which he cannot effectively deal with. It also accompanies a lifestyle that is personified by a neat appearance, skill in verbal manipulation and an uncanny ability to stay out of serious trouble.

The Cool Cat often appears indifferent to the problems around him, as though he is insensitive to pain, frustration or death. He rarely allows his real inner feelings to surface, because they may reveal that he is more sensitive to other people. The lifting of his protective shield would make him appear timid, and, therefore dilute his image. The Street Institution has trained him to act in this manner, to be cool, stern, impersonal in the face of all kinds of adversities. (p. 40)

Of course the transition from Regular to Cool Cat was neither as sudden nor absolute as described above. The description was intended as a thumbnail sketch roughly explaining the major shift in orientation recounted at the close of "Big Fame." It was not offered as an oil masterpiece depicting the full range of shades and hues accompanying the overall transformation. The interplay of school culture and street mores would continue to be a drama of rather intense ambivalence for me, as will be reported later. More important at this juncture is to develop a further sense of how this type of tension may guide the actions of other student-citizens and, consequently, those of people who propose to teach them in school.

Marva's Way

In 1975, after resigning from the Chicago school system, Marva Collins founded a school that since has been the object of much national attention. The school, Westside Prep, was featured on *60 Minutes* and was the subject of a television docudrama. Fortunately, a book has followed (Collins and Tamarkin 1982), which both focuses on Collins's pedagogy and serves as a valuable field study of a Black educational community. Many of the plaudits Collins has received are no doubt well deserved. Nonetheless, I do have reservations about what goes on in that unique educational environment.

One cannot seriously question the academic achievement per se that has taken place at Westside. When the students were tested in 1979 by an outside administrator, they scored higher and had progressed more than any other group tested. And tests alone, of course, could not tell the whole story. Gains in general awareness, confidence, and pride were also in evidence. By reading the myths, the fables, the Washington Irving, the Dostoyevsky, the especially beloved Shakespeare, in short, all the *literature* Collins had insisted they all read, the children had experienced remarkable academic and intellectual growth, had become able and, most importantly, *willing* to express opinions in formal settings. But the testing program could give no clue as to how much of themselves (or their *selves*) they chose not to reveal or how those decisions affected them. Such was not the purpose of the testing. However, one might expect Collins herself, as a self-proclaimed progressive educator, to be extremely concerned about a possible clash of value systems. But such does not appear to be the case.

While it is demanded of these children that they become avid readers of the classics, they are not, strangely enough, encouraged to read Black classics. Collins fails to include any on the official reading lists. Dickens is all right. And Tennyson is "in" along with Spenser, Aristophanes, and Thoreau. But there is no mention of Zora Neale Hurston, Ralph Ellison, Toni Morrison, Gwendolyn Brooks, or Richard Wright. Collins specifically ridicules Wright's *Black Boy* (1945/1966), recognized widely as a masterpiece. She claims it is too violent (though it's not as explicitly so as the *Macbeth* she cherishes) and that her students already have been exposed to enough of that type of writing. In discussing a passage from *Black Boy* along with other curriculum materials, Collins asserts that "all that 'relevance' undermines the very purpose of an education" (p. 156).

It remains beyond my comprehension how anyone's education can be undermined by exposure to Wright's autobiography, which shows a character so thirsty for book knowledge he seeks to devise a way to sneak volumes from the library. Wright phrases his predicament clearly:

> There was a huge library near the riverfront, but I knew that Negroes were not allowed to patronize its shelves any more than they were the parks and playgrounds of the city. I had gone into this library several times to get books for the white men on the job. Which of them would now help me to get books? And how could I read them without causing concern to the white men with whom I worked? I had so far been successful in hiding my thoughts and feelings from them, but I knew that I would create hostility if I went about this business of reading in a clumsy way. (pp. 267–68)

One might expect that the conservatism voiced by the strong disapproval of some of the very best in Black literature would also be expressed by a policy of eradicationism with respect to Black English. Collins is indeed consistent in this regard. As she addresses the class one day: "Children, listen to me for a moment. To succeed in this world, you must speak correctly. I don't want to hear any jive talk in here or any of this stuff about black English. You must not think of yourselves as black children or ghetto children. You must become citizens of the world, like Socrates" (p. 30). Obviously she didn't point out that there isn't any such language called worldcitizenese. Collins later offers a further explanation of her beliefs about language instruction: "The experts claim that correcting an inner-city child's grammar will damage his or her identity. I believe that not correcting grammar will damage that child's whole life. While others lowered their standards for inner-city students, I made mine higher" (p. 185).

There are at least four conceptual weaknesses evident in this passage. First, to make light of how bound up language is with identity represents a definite shortsightedness. That much should be clear by now. Second, one should know that despite attempts to "correct" children's grammar, children themselves for the most part *choose* which language varieties they will speak. Third, choosing to speak Standard English has been no guarantee that one would not be "damaged." The emptiness of the eradicationists' argument is revealed by the reality that (a) generations of Black English speakers have been subjected to "correction" programs that haven't worked and (b) their contemporaries who have mastered Standard English still have faced inordinate struggle in trying to "succeed." And fourth, it is misleading to explain the achievement at Westside as the result of standards set as opposed to standards negotiated. Such explanation begs the question of active student compromise.

Perhaps the sternest test of Collins's approach came when she ran a city-sponsored summer program for elementary school students (relatively unpromising ones) from Chicago's notorious Cabrini-Green housing projects. Of the 140 children who began the program, 87 finished, and in the process they demonstrated significant gains in language skills. On the other hand, 53 students (38 percent) dropped out of the program. These are the mixed results some observers would anticipate from a public program in which Horatio Alger and universalist mythologies are heavily pushed. Many students will buy into them, but a large number, recoiling from value conflicts, will not. Note how close the 38 percent drop-out rate is to the 40 percent failure rate Colin Greer (1976) claims is a built-in feature of most public educational programs.

This is not to say that Marva Collins is no better than the average public school teacher. After all, she specifically requested Cabrini-Green's "worst" and did, in my estimation, a more than creditable job. She's no miracle worker, a tag the media have often given her, but she is a fine teacher. She would be an even better one and would reach even more students if she toned down the proselytizing a bit and allowed more of the children's street experiences, particularly their language, to have legitimate functions in the classroom. Such experiences could be a starting point for crucial and truly enriching discussions, as opposed to superficial teacher-dominated ones, of relationships among language, knowledge, culture, identity, politics — in brief, many of the connections Black children often ponder. If her students can read Shakespeare and toss about polysyllabic words for effect, then they can participate in such a forum.

With all the skill, dedication, and commitment to Black people that Collins possesses, it seems a sad irony that she doesn't realize that it is the sum of her loving and her Blackness that allows her to spout convincing universalist rhetoric to those children she does reach. They trust her. However, her pedagogy is not one to put in the hands of those who won't work as hard, love as much, or can't be as Black. I feel safer recommending that teachers wishing to turn young Blacks into mimics and scholars of Shakespeare should be prepared to engage in a more far-ranging than usual discussion of Ferdinand's assertion: "I am the best of them that speak this speech/Were I but where 'tis spoken" (*The Tempest*, act 1, sc. 2).

Thirty-seven Learners

The memoirs of Herbert Kohl (1968) also provide an important outlook concerning the education of inner-city Blacks. Kohl describes his work with a sixth-grade class in Harlem during the 1962–63 academic year, the same year I would have been a fifth grader in Harlem if my family hadn't moved. I missed exposure to the stern suppression and harmful neglect that Kohl understood to be characteristic of the system there. His thirty-six pupils understood it too:

> I took the children to the Teachers College cafeteria where we sat and had lunch. Not that people didn't stare and sit uncomfortably next to us. Marie sat down next to me and asked: "Who they think they are anyway, rolling their eyes at us?" I explained to her that the people she saw were training to become teachers. She smiled and nodded. That explained the hostility and coldness. (p. 121)

But although the Harlem school system generally was in no better shape than the one Kozol encountered in Boston, it wasn't nearly as restrictive with respect to the actions of individual teachers. One could be as creative as one dared to be. Given such autonomy, Kohl and his students conducted a workshop in humanistic education.

Kohl stresses throughout his book the importance of the teacher as receptor and, most important, how he took his own advice. He entertained matters of concern to the students, matters like their ghetto habitat and their peculiar problems. He listened, without prescribing a particular manner of speaking, to the stories of their lives. Even though there is little one teacher can do substantially to change many lives, there is, as I hope to have made clear so far, great value in encouraging the discussion of community experiences within academic environs. As Kohl explains in his own words: "I could do nothing about the facts, therefore my words were useless. But through listening, the facts remained open and therefore placed school in the context of the children's real world" (p. 45).

Once the children gained full confidence that the classroom was a place where much of what perplexed them could at least be aired, if not ironed out, they became tremendously enthusiastic about school. They read voraciously as Kohl made available plenty of literature, myths, and other items of personal interest. And, as in my own case, all this reading enhanced their productive language capacities. Particularly impressive was their writing: deep, provocative, sometimes humorous. Many of them wrote prolifically, often producing texts in excess of three thousand words. Set in the context of what some of them were accomplishing, my own poetry and essay experiments were nothing at all unusual — or remarkable.

During the course of the term the students as a whole demonstrated significant gains on standardized IQ tests and seemingly miraculous gains on standardized reading tests, though they viewed the exams as necessary evils. Both the thirty-six students and Kohl knew that the crucial work had taken place within the classroom environment, which all thirty-seven of them had worked vigorously to endow with meaning. Kohl summarizes the experience:

> The children learned that they could do unpleasant but necessary work; they also knew that the test preparation was not all there was to education, that the substance of their work, the novels and stories, the poems and projects they created, were the essential thing no matter how the external world chose to judge them. They were proud of their work and themselves. I felt thrilled and privileged to teach them and witness them create. I offered what I could to them; they offered much in return. I am grateful that over the course of the year I could cease to be afraid and therefore respond to what the children had to teach me of myself, of themselves and the world they lived in and we shared as human beings. (p. 178)

Unfortunately, one year's experience could not ensure further progress for these students in formal education. For as they went forward into junior high school they once again entered classrooms in which their lives were not regarded seriously, where their language once again was subjected to attempts at eradication. Some of the students who ventured into predominantly White schools outside of Harlem soon expressed a desire to leave those institutions. They had not enjoyed the intense competition.

In certain ways the most interesting graduate of Kohl's class was Grace, who had been the most academically advanced by far. Grace, one who could relish the competition, was the only one of the thirty-six children to make a special progress class. She subsequently did so well that upon graduation from junior high school, she was in a position to turn down her acceptance at the prestigious Bronx High School of Science, opting instead, as beneficiary of a hefty scholarship, for an exclusive prep school in New England. Her letters to Kohl, which spanned a period of several years, were little more than straightforward progress reports of her success. Kohl was thus prompted to remark:

> Now Grace is in her second year in a New England Prep School. She fits wholly neither there nor at home in Harlem. She is one of the "school Negroes," a gifted one but still an anomaly. The other students are as open as possible, and she has made several sincere friends. Yet to live simultaneously in two worlds, a rich white one and a poor black one, is to be fully part of neither. Grace has become alienated from Harlem, her home, her friends, her very self, in attempting to be a part of the prep school world. But she can't fully participate there; she's too poor, too lonely, too much of a special case. It is hard to know what will come of her alienation, whether it will pull her apart or whether she will transcend it and show us adults a way to synthesize the contradictions we make and allow in our society. (p. 223)

Grace's dilemma was very similar to the one I encountered and to that faced by Richard Rodriguez (1983). I wonder if eventually she became rebellious (more like myself) or continued to chase the Dream (more like Rodriguez). Phrased another way, in sociolinguistic terms, it is a question of whether she has used her pain to criticize eradicationist policy or to affirm it.

While there are many other closely related studies that can be cited along with those above, I think the educational experiments I have chosen to report here fairly well represent the range of classroom situations in which Black students find themselves; that is, despite adjustments for the ethnicity and gender of the instructor, virtually all classrooms can be imagined as functioning somewhere between the open approach used by Kohl and the rigid method employed by Collins. Approaches strongly resembling Kohl's certainly seem superior.

Reconsidering Labov's Lames

Before closing this chapter I will quickly shift focus from classroom practices to field research in order to examine briefly some aspects of the research Labov (1972) reported under the title of "The Linguistic Consequences of Being a Lame." Such examination will underscore the major themes I have so far brought to the surface, namely, the self as a dynamic system, the linguistics of selfhood, and the interrelationships among school and street cultures. In addition, analyzing Labov's work serves as a good lead-in to the final segment of the narrative, which will even further highlight these issues.

Labov generally has conducted outstanding research with respect to Black English, having provided arguably the finest linguistic descriptions of the dialect, given cogent explanations of the vernacular relative to reading and oral skills, and exhibited an understanding of the cultural and political tensions that help divert the interest of Black English speakers from the schools to the streets. However, his explication of the transactions occurring in the street environment itself leaves much to be desired, mostly because he makes too direct a connection between "hipness" and the level and frequency of Black English contained in one's speech. Having worked among a few select gangs in Harlem, who as a whole often spoke the lowest-prestige form of Black English, Labov concludes that these youngsters were more streetwise or "down" than a group of kids he identified as squares or, in the vernacular, lames. But since he made no detailed observations of these so-called lames, one is left to wonder why he draws this conclusion with so much conviction.

Labov, being a lame himself, was susceptible to being fooled by any Regular or Cool Cat who wished to entertain him, especially when his method of study was suspect to begin with. He has usually insisted that language is studied most validly if one has access to normal social discourse. Witness his own comments:

> We focus upon natural groups as the best possible solution to the *observer's paradox:* the problem of observing how people speak when they are not being observed. The natural interaction of peers can overshadow the effects of observation and helps us approach the goal of capturing the vernacular of everyday life in which the minimum amount of attention is paid to speech: this is the most systematic level of linguistic behavior and of greatest interest to the linguist who wants to explain the structure and evolution of language.
>
> But there is a second even more compelling reason for us to select natural groups of speakers rather than isolated individuals. The vernacular is the property of the group, not the individual. (p. 256)

Labov indeed followed his own prescription when he studied the gangs, but he studied the so-called lames by use of the formal interviewing technique he otherwise eschews. So while he speaks of the linguistic consequences of being a lame, and such consequences certainly are that many lames speak fairly standard English, we don't know if *his* analysis is based on the output of any real lames at all. He hasn't observed these youngsters well enough to make such a claim legitimately. He can only resort to making the case by definition and, as the description below shows, he has enough trouble trying to accomplish that. "They are less open to social pressures to fight, to steal, or take drugs. Of course some lames steal, shoot up, and drop out; but as a group they have a better record" (p. 285). Uncertain about what a lame really is, Labov is reduced to offering group comparisons, which, besides being contradictory, still can't tell us how *he knows* who specifically is or is not a lame.

The chance that Labov was put on to a great extent is very real. He left himself open to the possibility by failing to be as diligent of method as he probably desired to be. There were shrewd youngsters out there who were not in traditional gangs but were, nonetheless, fashioning and reinforcing and projecting intricate selves through complex manipulations of Black English and Standard English. By overromanticizing the basilect often heard in the street clubs and viewing the language of the so-called lames as diametrically opposed to that of the gang members, Labov may have missed an opportunity to describe those intriguing processes. If he understands the game of the streets half as much as he professes to, he must know that in streetball, as in basketball or football, the ability to fake deftly to the right and then go left is a much valued skill. It allows a person to choose to a large degree how predictable he or she is. It makes one difficult to judge.

8
Valedictory

I

Regardless of the fact that I had qualified for an S.P. class, school officials had me ticketed for Junior High School 16 in Corona, which didn't even have such a class. But my mother wasn't going for that move and she freed me before the end of the first week. Getting out was the easy part. The main problem was where to go from there. Following my sister was the most appealing choice to me. No such luck. I was shipped down to William Cowper Junior High School in Maspeth. I was among the first wave of Black students sent to that school and, through the same zoning maneuver, so was the other half of the new dynamic duo, Wallace Jones.

My mother's brother, Uncle Howard, came through for me big. He had managed to gain a pretty steady hand in the real estate business by then and was intent on seeing to it that his nephew began junior high school on a fashionable note. He bought me a pair of Italian shoes, a mandatory fashion item; a pair of black ripple-soles, which were worthy of added compliment; and a pair of brown suede crepe soles, a definite eyebrow raiser. And I received a good supply of pants, shirts, socks, underwear, and handkerchiefs. I would have liked a couple of expensive, status-symbol knit sweaters, but I was never one to overload a gift horse's back.

Moms didn't appear overly grateful for what her brother had done, but I certainly was—had a great start toward a better than average wardrobe. That was important for a soul brother, a name a lot of us were beginning to call ourselves. You could obtain respect simply by dressing well.

In other words, you could get over better if you "vined." Get more attention from the soul sisters. Avoid some types of initiation. Evade becoming a laughingstock. Of course if you were just a plain bad MF you could get respect also. I preferred to try to earn it with style.

The classroom situation wasn't anything to worry about. When I arrived at Cowper, the two-year S.P. class was reportedly full and I was assigned to a three-year class. My mother had an urge to protest this move also, but then decided, with me in agreement, that the three-year program wouldn't be so bad after all. She probably recalled Sherry's misadventure. As for myself, I wasn't too keen on the idea of making up a grade on my sister anyway. I didn't want to become an embarrassment for her, you know, let her keep her place.

A 65 was generally the minimum passing grade in school, but in S.P. we were told that our minimum passing grade was 85. Marks below 85 on our report card would be circled with red ink as a reminder that they were below expectation. Consistent scoring below 85 was grounds for termination. I wasn't frightened in the least by such requirements. I felt I could score as highly as I wanted.

I had a soul brother and sister in the class. First Blacks that sat in a classroom with me since the first grade. Karen Owens was so cute I couldn't drum up enough nerve to speak to her much, though she was always nice enough. Danny Baylor and I clicked right away. He was from near the home neighborhood, down in East Elmhurst, and liked to talk as much as I did. He vined pretty well, even had a few knits. He was a little short on street savvy, but I had lots to give. And he could take or leave the White boys just as I could. So we were cool, would sit around and poke fun at our classmates who wore highwater pants, Beatles boots, Nehru shirts, and saturated their hair with Brylcreem; or others who followed the school regulation of wearing a tie every day and ran the same pair of cheap charlie pants for a week. It was a major offense for a brother to run a pair of pants, but it seemed standard procedure for several of our classmates. Danny and I didn't realize that some of their parents had already socked away plenty toward college tuition.

I started the term well but began to falter after only a few weeks. I couldn't keep my mind functioning right, wouldn't concentrate, didn't seem interested. Wouldn't raise my hand much, wouldn't do my work thoroughly. All the ability I had to play the school game was failing to manifest itself.

Only Math seemed to motivate me. That algebra Mrs. Friedman was teaching us posed puzzles that never failed to seduce. Other classes were very boring by comparison. Even Science, with the experiments with magnets; even Spanish, which was new and should have captivated. A danger was near. I could feel it but just couldn't define it, couldn't get the tangled web of personality and environment to unravel into anything comfortable and clear.

One thing that was clear, but uncomfortable, was that there were too many rules. Those ties every day, baggy blouses for the girls, no turtlenecks for the guys, walk to the right of the thick red line in the hall, never intersect the thick red line in the hall, use the up staircase for going up, the down staircase for going down, line up in the yard, line up in the hall, sit tight in the auditorium, stay confined during lunch period. This brand of regimentation had no redeeming value I could see, so I viewed those rules as simply something to break, a decision that introduced me to a variety of disciplinary methods. If you didn't wear a tie, for example, which I hardly ever did, you had to print the word "tie" on a piece of paper and fasten this paper tie to a button of your shirt. I saw some guys use more paper on ties than they used on homework. I was almost in that category myself.

But even such nonsense as this wasn't supposed to affect me inside the classroom itself. I could always handle a classroom even when I could handle nothing else. I could excel beyond all interference. I hoped I was experiencing a temporary case of listlessness, that's all.

On the first report card my marks hovered in the 80s, with the exception of a 92 in Math and a 95 in Gym. That I had to improve was simple enough to see. Wallace Jones, however, was perplexed. Holding a nifty collection of mostly 65s in his hand, it was hard for him to accept someone drawing a bold red circle around so admirable a mark as an 80. I didn't bother to explain that I should have been getting at least 90 in every subject. Not after he said he was glad he only failed one thing.

Moms had a perplexing moment also. The smooth brow became wrinkled as she scanned the report. She squinted at each unexpected grade. But her only words were a flat "you can do better." Certainly I could. I just didn't.

One morning in late November I was leaving the bakery across Grand Avenue after stocking up on some beloved crumb buns. I would hide these in my desk and sneak munches during my early classes. Wallace was running over from the soda shop, dodging cars along the way, with a piece of news fresh off the grapevine.

"Hey Keith, I got a dynamite jump off. Hooky party, man."

"Yeah?" I was immediately interested. I had a couple of rounds of hooky under my belt by then. But only light stuff, you know, like hopping the 7 train into Manhattan to explore Times Square. Hooky parties, from what I heard, were the big leagues.

"Yeah man" Wallace continued. "This dude Benjamin I know is givin it. Be some older people there, ninth graders and stuff. Be a good chance to git your thing wet."

That was definitely a worthwhile concern. Wallace said there were only dry guys and wet guys. The wetter the better. And he was super eager to be among the best. I knew my good friend Mr. Shortside would be very fond of Wallace Jones. I had my own bashfulness to contend with of course, but I knew I had to try to beat it as soon as possible.

"Well I'll tell you Wallace, that does sound pretty dyno to me."

"Damn right it's dyno. That means you ready then, hunh?"

"I'm ever ready, just like the battery. Where is this party? Let's go."

"We gotta go back out the way, man. Down on 35th Avenue. Benjamin got a nice crib. Got upstairs and downstairs and a finished basement. It's perfect for partyin. How a day in school sound up against that?"

"Sounds like nothin to me. What you think it gon sound like? I said I'm down."

"Yeah O.K. But there's one thing you have to do first before you can git all the way down."

"Oh yeah? What's that?"

"Give up halfa dem crumb buns."

I tossed him the bag and we took off for the bus stop. Had the old blood racing again. A chill wind pinned my ears back and momentarily cloaked me in a shiver.

The set at Benjamin's was cool, just as Wallace had kept forecasting. As soon as I got there I knew I had indeed reached the big time. The voices of Smokey Robinson and Little Anthony spun out from the hi-fi. A couple rubbed together passionately in the most basic of dances. The aroma of pancakes shared the air with the smell of marijuana. Bacon shriveled up in sharp contrast to expanding natures. Sugar was passed along with sugar, and lemons were squeezed along with fresh young girls. The grits were thick like my throat.

Wallace hadn't told me that he had a buck-toothed beauty named Shirley awaiting his arrival, that the information about the party had actually been relayed to him as a message from her. After she was introduced to me, she was tugged by Wallace over to the sofa. I retreated to the hi-fi to thumb through the stack of 45s and pull off one of the classic maneuvers of an overly self-conscious young fellow. I became the disc jockey.

After awhile, after everyone had played their openings, the great Benjamin himself assumed center stage. He was a highschooler already, hot on the trail of some wild eighth grader. He was clad in slippers and a robe, endowed with authority.

"Yo everybody" he boomed. "I got too many here. I don't wanna bust no bubbles or nuffin but some of yall gotta go. And like I don't really wanna be kickin out nobody, but like I really didn't do all this invitin myself from the git, you know. We fixin to have like a serious thing here, like a couples thing. This ain't no babysittin operation or no place for no lames. So I ain't really pointin out nobody, but some of yall know yall ain't qualified to hang out here. So dig, rather than to hafta be peepin hole cards, I'm gonna let yall go on and tip easy, you know. Like I said, I really don't wanna hafta be peepin no hole cards."

Wallace came over to tell me something I had already figured out, that I wasn't going to be able to disc jockey my way through this affair.

"Hey Keith, you gotta crack on one of them dames so you can hang on out."

"I would man. But I don't see nobody all that fly."

"That ain't nothin man. Who said they had to be fly? Shirley ain't all that fly, but what it mean?"

"Yeah Wallace, but a lot of these broads probably ain't droppin no drawers yet anyway."

"Yeah well that's what you're here for, to git em started. Don't be scared Keith. All you hafta do is pull one off to the side and explain how you diggin her. Your style is hip enough you know."

"I know man, but see it's a th— —"

"Who you with man?" Benjamin had cut me off.

"I came here with Wallace."

"No little man, not like that. Is you got a squeeze or what? You know we ain't havin no deadbeats here. Not no nigguhs. Maybe you'll see a sister git away with it cause it might be the only way to keep another broad around. But ain't no nigguhs can git away with it."

I started to tell him that I hadn't really planned on staying, you know, that I was only killing a few minutes before I had to go take care of some other more serious business. Wallace's tongue, however, was quicker than mine.

"But check it out Benjamin, like this is my cousin Keith and he's kinda new around here and don't really know that many people yet. But my brother, see, he say he wanna see Keith git in the groove, you know. And he say you a good man to see about that. You know how you and P.J. is."

"Oh yeah. Me and P.J. is boss." He stepped back to look me over. "So you a cuz of P.J. hunh? Me and him is pretty tight. Done a lotta solids for each other. So tell P.J. not to worry about your H.O. card no more. I'm gon make you a lil tiger just like Wallace. But first you gotta start off right by gittin your head right and then you can go from there."

He yanked a nickel bag of reefer and a pack of Bambu from a pocket of his robe. I put down the records I was holding and accepted the gift casually.

"Bust it all the way down if you wanna" he advised. "You my man."
He turned and walked away. Wallace was elated.

"Benjamin's gon be all right with you now Keith. You gittin reefer like this. You never had none before, did you?"

"Naw man. I missed that time Big Rob was turnin everybody on. I know I can handle it though."

"Probably can. Ain't no big thing nohow. I'd git down with you but Shirley got some herself. I don't know. I'll still come check you out later."

"Yeah all right, if I'm not hooked up into something else."

When Benjamin was satisfied there weren't any more hole cards that needed to be peeped, he directed the remaining couples, only six, to various love nests about the house. I was stranded in the living room of course, but there were two sisters stranded with me. They were sitting on the sofa appearing decent to the eye and truly provocative to the mind. And with the marijuana as my crutch and possible advantage, I embarked on confused pursuit. I sank into the matching chair and set the reefer and Bambu down on the table before me.

"I know you sisters down with this, ain't yall?"

"Yeah we smoke" answered the "healthy" one with hair that fell down her back in a single long braid. Even though she was seated I could tell she already had hips her parents couldn't trust.

"That's good then. We can all smoke together. What's yall's names?"

"Mine is Chrystal."

"Helen." She was dark and had long unstraightened hair that fell loosely over her shoulders. She wasn't quite as jock as Chrystal, but I considered her prettier. She had a small, distinct face. Bright eyes. Didn't seem to belong there.

"What's your name?" asked Chrystal.

"Well everyone calls me just plain old Keith. That's my proper name."

We all beamed. I didn't figure to make any errors with the small talk; I just had to solve the problem of the reefer. Not the smoking part, I knew I would eventually get around to that. The rolling up of the joints was what I was most worried about, you know, how to get the girls to do it without me losing face. I had an idea how it was supposed to go but was sure my attempt would come up clumsy and expose me for the rank amateur I was. I didn't know there were plenty potheads who were lousy rollers.

"I don't want to trouble you sisters, but I jammed my finger playing basketball in the gym yesterday. If one of you knows how to roll, you can help me out a lot."

"Ah shucks, that ain't no problem" Chrystal assured me. "Both of us know how to roll good."

The girls expertly rolled up three quick joints; Helen produced a sporty chrome lighter and we began to get high. I inhaled too much at first and coughed violently. I told the girls I had a cold and made a pact with myself to be smoother. And as I got my technique down pat, more of a soft swallow, I expected my head to feel funny, you know, experience some kind of floating sensation. What I got instead was an invisible hand vigorously tickling my ribs causing a giddiness that was threatening to blow my cool. I managed to keep my jaws tight though, and kept on puffing, concentrating on my rap, adding a year or two to my age and a couple of female admirers to my past. We also talked of the relative demerits of our schools, and we identified a number of common acquaintances, yet avoided the reason everyone was supposed to be there at the party. We compared opinions on all the popular songs and singers and of course I kept the music spinning all the while. I was feeling really comfortable for the first time since Wallace had tracked me down that morning, didn't even mind if Chrystal and Helen caught me staring at them, didn't shy away when our eyes met. Everything was mellow. And I was on my third joint when the big break came.

Helen decided to go to the store. Reefer and I instantly interpreted the move as a seductive ploy by Chrystal. Figured this was how they worked their show, so when Helen left we immediately accepted the invitation.

"So come on" Reefer and I said as we sat next to her on the sofa and tried to embrace her.

"What's wrong with you boy?" she shot back, eluding our attempt and springing up from the couch.

"What you mean Chrystal? Ain't nothin wrong. I just well, I mean, well, uh, you know the scoop."

"Boy, ain't no scoop here! What, are you crazy or somethin?"

"No I'm not crazy. You know you really wanna git down, don't you?"

"Hell no nigguh! What makes you think I came here for that? Who you been talkin to?"

"Nobody. It's just—"

"Just nothin. You better leave me alone. That's what you better do. . . . What makes you think I like you anyway?"

"Nothin. Nothin." Reefer and I were wondering why such tantalizing breasts would change their mind. But though we were bewildered, we knew better than to press the issue and cause a ruckus that undoubtedly would lead to our ultimate embarrassment. We had little choice but to accept the setback. There was, however, some measure of consolation. I could at least prove to Wallace that I tried. And I later found out, though he hid the truth for awhile, that mere trying was as far as Wallace had gotten with his girl. He finally admitted that she had come up lame on him.

II

I spent the Christmas recess at Uncle Howard's house out in Cambria Heights, tucked in near the Nassau County line, a couple of rungs up the ladder of aspiration from Corona. Uncle Howard's place was a good visit for me, especially when I got to go alone. Then he and Aunt Ruby and my twelve-year-old cousin, Stephanie, could direct all their attention my way. Aunt Ruby even let me set the dinner menu most evenings, and I was able to achieve the exhilaration of watching someone prepare meat loaf rather than chicken for the simple reason that I decided they would do so.

Stephanie had a taste for adventure and mystery. She was a natural freak for Nancy Drew and Huck Finn and Alfred Hitchcock. But her favorite was me. So after she was sworn to secrecy and properly warned not to get any ideas, I would fill her head with embellished accounts of my latest exploits and observations. Stephanie would sit amazed, soaking in everything forever.

Her life was bland, which was fine with me as I thought the bland life was ideal for her. I was happy to see that Uncle Howard and Aunt Ruby were very particular about the types of kids she hung around with. All squares. There was this brother in the other three-year class, Donald Anderson, who was treated that way. He didn't vine too well and usually sat off by himself in the cafeteria, like maybe he was a little uppity. I was the only one of the "in crowd" who ever approached him, and I immediately discovered that there wasn't anything snobbish about him at all. As cousin Stephanie did, he had to live inside a square. And I figured the square was enabling him to excel in class.

I would fantasize, then, about being like Donald Anderson and cousin Stephanie. It would never last too long, though, before I snapped to my senses and realized all over again that a square's life just wouldn't do. I remained grateful for the relative freedom with which I was entrusted, even wanted more.

One night during my visit, after Stephanie had finally put me down in favor of bed, I was in the kitchen reading a magazine article about Martin Luther King Jr., who had just that month received the Nobel Peace Prize. He was the youngest man ever to win that award and that seemed quite a feat to me. Naturally I had to find out all I could about how he had become so respected so quickly.

Uncle Howard came in for some ice. According to him, late television and sipping scotch, lightly sipping scotch, was a great combination. His eyes twinkled and he flashed his amusing grin. He had the manly version of the face my mother wore when she was happy.

"Hey Keith, what are you reading about now?"

"Oh this is only a little article about King winning that Nobel Peace Prize."

"Yeah isn't that something Keith? Just goes to prove what I tell folks all the time. The man is a great leader. This is something for the soul brothers to be proud of, don't you think?"

"I guess so Uncle Howard. He must really be something to get a prize like that." I was far more concerned with King's fame than I was with his politics, but I liked to admire him the right way for my uncle.

"He is that" my uncle replied. "He's doing a good job getting the brothers and sisters their rights."

"Yeah, a lot of people think he's loquacious just for show. But that's not how it is."

"Loquacious hunh? Runnin off at the mouth. I like that. That's your word already or you just picked it out of the magazine? I know it's probably yours."

"Yeah I already knew it, but it's not really that big a word. It really ain't no big thing."

"Yes it is too. You got a good head for the books. Stephanie's like that. She's pretty good. But not as good as you. Not quite. You can be about the best, that is, if you want to be."

"Yeah? Well I always want to do well."

"Oh I'm not so sure about that now. I used to be, but I don't know now . . . and I've been meaning to talk to you about it anyway."

Uncle Howard finished plunking cubes into his glass. He returned the tray to the freezer and sat opposite me at the table. He spoke slowly. "Well Mr. Keith, your mother says you aren't doing as well in school as you might."

"When did she say all that?"

"One night on the telephone. It wasn't any big production. I was just asking about you and your sisters and she said you could be doing better than you were."

"What, she said I was doing bad?"

"No she didn't say all that, only that you should be doing better. New school isn't too rough for you, is it?"

"No it's not all that rough. I didn't get such a hot report card but I'm doing a whole lot better right now. You'll see."

He jumped up from the table, sipped the excess water from his glass. "You know Keith, it's your world baby. Stick with those books and they'll take you places. You and Sherry and Stephanie, all yall. That's a big break too because when I was comin up there wasn't any guarantee we could attend school. Man, I had to miss two whole years to work and help your grandmother. By the time I got back I was in the same class as your mother. I must admit it was a blessing though. Your mother's the one who pulled me through. She was the sharp one. That's why, uh, well, uh, well forget that. Just look. I don't have a lot of brains but I got a lot of hustle. I'm merely out here tryin to do as well as the next man. I think I'm doing all right, don't you?"

"Yeah Uncle Howard. You're doing real well."

"Well you gonna do even better. You keep at those books like you're supposed to and you keep your spirits up. Don't get caught up in the wrong crowd out there. It's like driving, keep your eyes on where you have to go. I understand that it's a little rough over that way, and there's a lot of guys you probably see who aren't as interested in the right things as you are. But don't be a follower or anything like that. Go for yourself. I know you. You see things pretty quick to be so young. So keep seeing good and go for yourself." He jingled his glass of ice and drank off the excess water again. "Hey Keith" he resumed. "Remember baby, it's gonna be your world."

"Yeah. I'll remember that."

"Okay then. Let me go on up and sip this scotch. Not to get intoxicated you must understand. I just like to sip. See you in the morning."

Uncle Howard, as it turned out, had a notion about seeing me every morning, you know, like a permanent custody thing. Moms wouldn't even entertain the idea. I didn't catch the conversation, but whatever was said put a strain on their relationship for awhile. Plus Moms said that Uncle Howard was a drunken fool.

Malcolm went down in a hail of bullets right about then. I really didn't think they would get him. When they bombed his home, Wallace and I walked over to survey the damage. I thought some people were simply putting the scare on him. I had a hunch, obviously a poor one, that they wouldn't close him all the way out.

I took this news harder than I had taken the Kennedy tragedy fifteen months earlier, although this was opposite the general reaction in Malcolm's own neighborhood. The heads were really hanging low after Kennedy's death, but Malcolm's demise didn't produce half as much grief. It was a hot topic for talk, however, and I heard enough opinions to be totally confused. I heard the communists were behind the assassination.

I heard it was the CIA. Others said it was some dope dealers because Malcolm had been fighting drug traffic up in Harlem. And of course folks were talking about the Muslims. The mosque uptown was set afire, and the one in Corona, which was only one block from my home, was being watched by a special police patrol.

Wallace Jones didn't seem to give much thought to the situation, was nowhere near as frightened or reflective or angry as I was. Maybe Uncle Howard had something there about quick eyes. Nonetheless, my feet were never any faster than Wallace's and we kept racking up adventures in tandem. Even had special ones for school.

They held an after school center in the boys' gymnasium. Wallace and I would shoot a few hoops, give things a chance to settle down, then slip from the gym to roam the rest of the school. Our favorite stop was the Home Economics classroom, where we often found a stash of cookies and fruit juices. Many of the cookies would be inedible, so we had a fierce scramble to see who could grab the majority of the edible ones. We saved the brick-hard ones for our own little discus throw competition.

We never found enough supplies to try to make our own batch, and Wallace said he was going to be the first male to enroll in Home Economics. I said if he made it I would follow. But both of us eventually had to content ourselves with Woodworking Shop.

Our most intense adventure that term was not planned, though it was more or less expected as White boy trouble was inevitable. The situation inside the school was calm enough, but the community at large was hostile and some of the older adolescents in the area were the ones who would transform this general hostility into specific physical incidents. There had been a few clashes up by the train station and on the bus, but Wallace and I had missed those gatherings. We had to face our encounter alone.

We were almost two hours late for school that morning because a hooky party had been canceled on us. Wallace had the crumb bun money, and after we got them, not being in any hurry at all, we crossed over to the soda shop and hoisted a couple of egg creams. When we emerged from the soda shop, four guys who looked like third-rate imitation Hell's Angels were at the bus stop apparently waiting for the bus to Ridgewood. I figured they were from Grover Cleveland High School, if they went to school at all. Wallace and I tried to ease by invisibly but didn't succeed. One of the boys casually ripped off a car antenna.

"Hey, you niggers got lotsa balls to be stragglin in like this. Ain't nobody to save your black asses. You know niggers need protection."

We quickened our step, poised to run. All we needed was the starter's pistol and Wallace fired it himself in the form of words.

"Yeah? So who protects yo momma then?" And we were off.

The White boys were just as ready to sprint as we were, but it was a simple case of the fox running for dinner while the rabbits were running for their lives. In a footrace such as this, Wallace and I simply could not be caught.

"Which gate Wallace?" I cried out as I was moving at top speed. Even with a few books in my arm I stayed right with him.

"Side one. First one." Wallace surged in front by half a step. We turned into the gate entrance and sped up the walkway to the door. It was locked. We tugged frantically at the handles and banged furiously on the heavy brown door until we were out of time. As we hit the gate entrance again our pursuers were just about there. Wallace pivoted better than Gale Sayers, hardly breaking stride as he turned down the block. I stumbled slightly and heard the whoosh of the antenna as it split the air just a fraction of a second behind my neck. Fear, fortunately, pulled me together rather than ripped me apart and I became a too—swift rabbit once again.

We almost ran through the next door before we even had time to stop to open it. We paused in the doorway, panting, watching their approach. They stopped short of the gate. Winded.

"Better hope we never catch you" gasped the bearer of the steel whip. "Whooo, a scared nigger sure knows how to run."

"So what sucker" I countered. "I see a punk ass honkie sure knows when to stop too."

"Oh yeah? We'll come in there and beat your asses for you."

"Oh yeah Joey?" cut in Wallace with his White boy imitation. "Beat my meat is what you'll do, you greasy pimple-faced bastard."

"Oh just listen to the wise asses now. Big talk on the run. We'll see if you make so heavy with the cracks this afternoon."

"Ah go suck an egg Joey. You ain't got the nerve."

"Oh no shitface?"

"Shitface? Hey be nice Joey. That ain't what your mother called me last night."

"Joey" started for the door. It was only a bluff but it was enough to send us deep into the shelter of the school and into the fortress of our own laughter.

Turned out their rumblings about that afternoon were mere bluff also. Too bad. There was about a score of young brothers out there hoping they were for real. Crowds had heart. Individuals had to be ever alert and speedy.

III

NASA was emerging from a lull. Astronauts were being sent up in pairs that spring. The second duo, McDivitt and White, was good for sixty-two orbits. Impressive. It felt good to relate to an old value.

School certainly wasn't getting my loyalty. I was mired in mediocrity, fortunate not to be doing much worse. Uncle Howard blamed my friends, my "bad influences." He said I was becoming too much of a follower. I didn't argue the charge, partly because I knew his mind was made up already. But I knew Uncle Howard didn't understand everything about following and leading, definitely didn't know how I handled Marty Rosenberger by myself.

When the term ended, Wallace once again praised my marks. He was especially impressed by my reading score, which was at a so-called eleventh-grade level, a full five grades above his.

My problem in school, to my teachers, was a lack of effort on my part. My problem, to me, was that I had simply had an off year. All people, even Mays and Mantle, were entitled to one.

That summer we played all the old fun back. Only major change in the format was the addition of a little Colt .45 malt liquor, a little Bacardi rum, a little Bali Hai wine, and a little herb. I now had marijuana and the General Electric Pavilion at the World's Fair joined together. I felt you would have to go a long way to top that. Oddly enough though, my personal highlight of the summer came when I was perfectly sober.

It was about as calm a Saturday afternoon as we could possibly have going. Just a little stickball game in the street. Without even any arguments. The sheer pleasure of guiding a bat powerfully and gracefully into the back of a rubber ball.

Everything was fine until I was summoned to the house to mop the kitchen floor. Now I never saw anything wrong with swinging a mop. It was even pleasurable at times, but during the middle of a totally serene game was not one of them. I was upset, so I became somewhat illogical. Instead of knocking out the task promptly as I usually did, I decided to sulk and procrastinate and generally get on my mother's nerves. I stood in the middle of the living room shuffling a deck of playing cards and introducing myself to some new boyfriend of Sherry's and trying to sound as hip as I could. I knew it wouldn't be long before my mother reacted.

"Boy, stop messin around and git in there and do that floor like I told you to." Objectively speaking, that was a reasonable command.

"Don't rush me" I dared to respond. "I'll do it when I get ready."

"What did you say?"

Now you hear many people ask this question rhetorically, you know, when they had indeed heard what had been said. In this case, however, I was sure my mother thought she was hallucinating. She needed reassurance, and I provided it with a voice that was strong and bold and unmistakably real.

"I said don't you rush me. That's all. I'll mop when I get good and ready to mop."

Moms trembled with anger and I winced mentally. She was going to come with her best—an old severed ironing cord.

The pain cut through my T-shirt like fire, covered my whole back and then flamed out to my arms. I squeezed my hands into the tightest fists I could possibly make, bracing to endure the assault without even the slightest whimper. With my own defiant inspiration and the pressure of Sherry's friend looking on I figured to have enough resolve to get through. Moms continued lashing away with that cord, trying to break me. Sherry's friend could only admire my toughness. Then, as my mother went to lash at my arms now folded up against my chest, her eyes met mine. Whatever she saw made her lashing lose its steam. She hit me a few relatively painless licks and stomped off into her bedroom and slammed the door. I couldn't bank on it, but I could sense she would never try to whip me again. I knew she could never make me cry again and, after all, what good is a beating without yells and screams and promises to do better?

"See. You really upset Ma now" Sherry accused. I thought she might be sympathetic toward me, but I should have known better.

"I didn't upset anybody" I snarled.

"You did!"

"I did not! Let me beat you with that ironing cord and then let's see who's the one that's upset."

"I'm not talkin about like that."

"I know you're not. And that's your main damn problem. You can't ever talk about nothin mean a goddamn."

I stormed off into the bathroom and latched the door behind me, leaned back against it. Sore, but wanting to howl with joy. I had a victory so immense and dangerous it couldn't all sink in just then. I moved to the mirror and proudly inspected my whelps. And naturally I had to check out those wonderful eyes. What was there besides plain old brown? I couldn't get it. I stretched them, squinted them, tried all the variations of my Sonny Liston glare. But I didn't see anything in them that would have startled or frightened or defeated me. It would have to come to me later. I had a floor to mop and I was determined to do a good job.

So that was the outstanding event that summer until a Black man who was drunk and driving was arrested by a White highway patrolman for drunken driving and the entire Watts district of Los Angeles exploded. Snipers and blazes and twenty thousand government troops and looting and machine guns and tear gas and bayonets and curfews. Thirty-four dead. Over one thousand injured. Over three thousand arrested. The most shocking incident I had seen on television yet. Even more shocking than the Harlem riots and the death of Oswald. It was, when I least needed it, another fiery decoration for my memory.

President Johnson denounced the Black rioters and said that just like the Ku Klux Klan they were destroyers of a free America. But President Johnson never sent twenty thousand troops against the Klan. He might occasionally restrain but he would never attack. You would never see three thousand Klansmen arrested. I felt that President Johnson shouldn't talk us into the same boat as the Klan if he never were actually going to put the Klan in the same boat with us. Wallace had it figured exactly the same way. We felt it was something any thirteen year old should understand.

IV

My off year was quickly becoming an off two years. I couldn't get my all-around academic game going, and early in the term I had a feeling, a rather indifferent one, that my time in S.P. was almost at an end. No one in my class thought I was dumb, however. They knew, as I did, that I simply didn't give as much of a damn as I should have. And since we all knew I could hang out with the "smart crowd" if I wanted to, proving myself to them was not important.

Danny Baylor was slipping badly also but wasn't any more concerned than I was, said he could take S.P. or leave it. And there were several White boys, such as David Greene and John Stark, who said they felt the same way. We were the rebels, the ones who had to be threatened with zeroes three or four times before we would at least temporarily simmer down. We were nowhere near as defiant and anti-school as Wallace Jones and some of my other friends, who couldn't be intimidated with sub-freezing marks, but we were a lot tougher to handle than, say, a John Sabo, who would blush with embarrassment if he were caught for so trivial an offense as gazing out of the window instead of focusing on the blackboard.

My math was still pretty decent, but English became my favorite class that year, partly because of the way we were challenged by Mrs. Applebaum. A model of confidence and class, she claimed she wasn't at all impressed by how intelligent we were alleged to be, would tell us, in fact, that we were vastly overrated. I felt personally offended. I mean teachers were always after me about discipline and effort, but none of them had ever directly questioned my capability — at least not convincingly. But Mrs. Applebaum had me on the ball for awhile, you know, for the sport of it. And though I didn't produce all she thought I should have, I absorbed more than she'll ever know. Gained my greatest understanding of the short story in general, of "unity of purpose." Enjoyed some particular stories such as "The Gift of the Magi." Although I fully understood how the story was viewed popularly as a tale of great love and selflessness, I also saw the work as confirmation of a dictum I had once heard my mother express: Love is an understanding between two fools. Mrs. Applebaum laughed and said that both my mother and I might make good literary critics.

I even let Mrs. Applebaum talk me into entering the oral recitation contest. I had read parts of "The Highwayman" so well in class that she thought I had an excellent chance to win the medal. She even volunteered to coach me after school. We would get the whole enchanting, beautifully lyrical poem to sound just perfect.

When I went to sign up for the contest I discovered that the selections had to be by American authors. No "Highwayman." I instantly decided not to compete but was later persuaded otherwise by Mrs. A. I wound up choosing some long patriotic poem by William Cullen Bryant, can't even remember the name of it, and in the contest I was totally outclassed by this girl named Vivian. She was definitely talented, no doubt about that. I mean she had even taken formal drama lessons and I wouldn't be surprised if she showed up on a Broadway stage one day. But I still feel I would have had a real good shot at that medal with "The Highwayman."

Mrs. Applebaum said she was proud of me because I had managed to come up with a good effort. Wallace Jones and company thought the contest was fixed. They were sure I had given the best "speech." But I knew better. Vivian truly deserved to win that award. But I didn't feel as though I had lost anything at all.

I guess that was the high point on the calm side that year. The wild side only grew wilder. Along with several other hustles, I mastered the art of "roughing off" money from some of the other kids, that is, obtaining cash through intimidation without the use of physical force. The key was to avoid actually "taking" the money to avoid ever being accused of theft. This was surely not a hustle for everyone. To be successful at the rough off game required great judgment (to pick the right mark), personality (to sell the bluff smoothly), and cunning (to leave the victim either feeling he had done you a favor of his own will or just plain afraid to tell). If you fumbled a rough off attempt you had to back off, fight, or maybe commit an out-and-out robbery. I may have backed off once or twice but on the whole I was as good as any artist in the school. I could have won a prize.

V

The guidance counselor for the eighth grade, Mrs. Gold, hopped on the bandwagon of those who would speak to me about my wasting good potential. But whenever I talked with her, her wording or logic or both seemed clumsy and she turned me off. There wasn't much guiding she could do for me.

Wallace got into a fight down in the cafeteria and my name became prominent during the ensuing investigation. I was summoned to Mrs. Gold's office — but not to give my account of matters. She was using the opportunity instead to sound off, to counsel, once again. She annoyed me immediately.

"Tell me something Raymond. Why do you hang around, let me say, with Wallace Jones?"

"Because he's my friend and next-door neighbor. I need more reasons than those?"

"No. No, those are good enough reasons I suppose. But why the others? Are they friends also?"

"You mean like Harry Jenkins and Thomas Warren? Yeah, they're my friends too."

"But why would you choose friends like that? You're not the same type of kid that they are. Just look, you're gifted enough to be an S.P. student and all. Doesn't that say something to you about the kinds of friends you should have?"

"Not really. I understand what you're saying, but I make friends with the people I like. And I don't think any of my friends are better than me and I don't think I'm better than any of them. Maybe you don't think they're ideal for me but, uh, but I'm not gonna worry myself too much about what you think anyway."

"Now relax Raymond. Just relax. I don't mean to upset you. I'm just concerned about your future. You can go a long way in life if you don't let anyone hold you back. I believe you are multi-talented and that there are all sorts of opportunities that can open up for you. Wouldn't your mother like to see you make something of yourself, become somebody special?"

"Of course she would, I guess."

"Well you can do it. But, like with anything important, it will take a fair amount of responsible effort."

"Yeah I know that. Can't expect to get something for nothing." I eased up on the counselor a little, gave her a little of what she wanted to hear.

"That's more or less it. And you have to have your mind set on the proper things, proper values. You know Raymond, and I don't mean to sound too ominous, but have you ever thought that a psychiatrist could help you?"

"Help me do what?" I replied while remaining cool.

"Help you solve some of your emotional problems. Again, excuse me if I sound ominous; I don't mean to imply that anything's terribly wrong with you. You're not crazy of course, but everyone has little problems from time to time. Don't you think so?"

"Yes, I imagine so. I know I have problems but I think I'll just solve mine by myself."

"If you can."

"Yeah, if I can. Even if I can't I'm not gonna worry too much about it now because really my main problem is becoming an adult. Once I get older, old enough, you know what I mean, then I'll be okay."

"I see. Would you be afraid to see a psychiatrist if I could arrange it? Naturally your mother would have to approve." I knew right then I would never have to worry about seeing one. Moms would think Mrs. Gold needed a psychiatrist for thinking I needed one.

"No I'm not afraid. I just don't think it's necessary. I can solve my own problems."

"Maybe so. Nevertheless I would like you to mention my suggestion to her. Will you promise to do that for me?"

"Sure. I'll mention it. I'll see what she says." I would mention it to my mother as a joke, and that's exactly how she would accept it.

In truth, Mrs. Gold's shrink talk did nag me for awhile, caused me to ponder how much control I had over myself, over my own life, you know, whether I was the player or the played. But I finally shrugged off all that heavy reflection and became all the more disgusted with the counselor, another do-good worrier who wouldn't understand that none of my peers had any combination of powers greater than my own. Not even Harry Jenkins, whom she thought was the most unsuitable company for me.

Now Harry was our leader in a sense, a head taller than the rest of us, always clowning around but had a real solid punch. In fact, Harry sometimes punched too well. He cracked a White boy's jaw that spring outside the subway station on Queens Boulevard. Got himself arrested by detectives who hung around the school for two days before they nabbed him.

Although I didn't see it all, I understood it as a little shoving match that only became a criminal matter because of the racial climate of the times and the fact that Harry hit so hard. There was no real right or wrong I could determine, only that it was right that Harry, like Louis and Ali, should win his fights. But the loser saw it very differently, saw himself as the victim of an unprovoked attack. So the issue had to be decided in court, a formal place, not such a good venue for the home team. First there would be an Information and Evidence Hearing, then maybe a trial.

I decided to help Harry, much to his delight, by volunteering to serve as a witness. Although I was pretty sure he was going to lose the case, I thought I could at least shorten the odds. I just knew I could handle myself in the courtroom much better than most of the others who said they would support him. I figured they would panic or freeze or overtell the story or walk into some verbal trap and contradict themselves. Or perhaps they would stare down at the floor too much, or get too hostile or hysterical, or sound too "street." Just telling the truth would never be quite enough. Only this White guy in Harry's class was a person I felt good about as a witness. I thought he was even better than me.

I dressed a bit preppy for the court hearing. Put on my bright yellow button-collar shirt with the red paisley print around the inside of the collar. My tie, which I searched far and wide for, precisely matched that fashionable blaze of a pattern.

Harry's lawyer thought the tie was fine. Said so when he introduced himself, had caught me, in my somber radiance, eyeing the bus from the Youth House that was parked out on 89th Avenue and seemed to take up too much of the street. Cars could barely squeeze by in a single file. The lawyer mentioned my appearance again before the judge, emphasized my clean-cut nature while he led me through a re-telling of my story.

The Corporation Counsel, the only other person in the room, which surprised me, had no compliments for me. Nor sympathy. He paced back and forth, clad properly in conservative tweed and standard cordovans. Lingered by the judge's bench, gave me plenty of time to get nervous, to stay in touch with the clamminess of my palms. His voice boomed as he began the cross examination.

"You say you saw Harry Jenkins push and then punch the plaintiff, Jonathan Craig. Is that correct?"

"No sir. That's not what I said. I said I saw the other boy push him first. Then I saw Harry push back; then the other boy pushed back harder, and then Harry punched him. *That* is what I said." I looked directly at him and kept my own voice loud, but well short of defiant.

"Oh I see" he countered. "I wasn't sure I understood. Then you did see Harry punch him in the face? Is that so?"

"Yes it is. I did see that. Just as I already said."

"I see. . . . Tell me, did you hear any nasty words exchanged between the two of them? Any racial insults?"

"You mean did I hear any derogatory stuff?" Boy did I stretch out that "derogatory." A one word poem.

"Uh, yes, uh, that's precisely what I mean. Did you hear anything of that nature?"

"No I did not."

"You didn't? Then you must be positive there was no such language used."

"No. I can't say that at all. As I said before, I was in the candy store when the whole thing started. I know some people are talking about hearing, uh, how do you say it? (I faked) Epithets? Yeah that's it. Epithets. I know some people are talking about that kind of stuff but I can't say anything about that at all. All I can be sure about is what I saw. I came out of the candy store and saw the other guy push Harry. Harry pushed him back, got pushed back hard, and then Harry punched him. That's what I saw." I tried to sound apologetic.

The Corporation Counsel suddenly waved toward the judge. "That's enough for me your Honor." And I was abruptly excused. Didn't get a chance to try to read the judge's face, get some feedback.

When I came back out into the waiting area I exchanged small talk with the other witnesses about "how it was." I then wandered again to the window overlooking the bus from Spofford and the deliberate cars easing down the road in the direction of King's Park.

In little more than an hour the case was resolved. The judge ruled that there wasn't enough evidence for the court to consider the matter further. Harry showed his joy by hugging or shaking hands or slapping five with all who had testified on his behalf. He was talking about throwing a party. His father was more restrained, but obviously as pleased, as though he too had been vindicated. I only caught a glimpse of Jonathan, his jaw still wired. But one couldn't tell from his expression if, on a legal level, he had won or lost. His dad, though, seemed distraught. I don't know; maybe the medical bills were too heavy.

VI

My last year of junior high was my worst one in terms of grades. I was warned several times that I might be dismissed from S.P., but that didn't happen. Besides, because of my test scores, I gained admission to Stuyvesant High, one of the Board of Education's special academic high schools. Even though the prospects may not have been so great, I was a candidate for redemption. Ninth grade was actually the freshman year of high school, and the grades received would appear on the transcript to be sent to any college to which I eventually applied. A 70 average for the freshman year was no way to make Harvard or Yale or some other top think tank.

Stuyvesant proved to be an apt metaphor. It was named after Peter Stuyvesant, that peg-legged, last colonial governor of New York who lost a leg on a colonizing raid through St. Martin. I wasn't ripping folks off for land, but the good leg/bad leg part was certainly me.

I was tuned in more and more to the streets, the ones I walked and the ones on fire in the news. After a traffic accident involving a White motorist and a Black pedestrian, there was a riot right on Northern Boulevard in the spring of 1967. Angry residents vandalized White-owned businesses that were repaired subsequently with money from the higher prices the rioters themselves had to pay. Something absurd about it, of course, but that's the way those things went down. And in matters of ghetto sociology, Corona stayed up to date.

Maybe the high school could save me. Maybe old peg leg peering down from the portrait in the lobby could show me how you handled obstacles with one leg. And I did come out of the blocks fairly well. Got excellent marks in Biology and Geometry. A few of my S.P. classmates had entered the school with me, and Eddie Goldstein and Marty Rosenberger from P.S. 149 were also on hand although, having chosen two-year S.P. programs, they were now juniors. We didn't get too close this time around. I mean nobody said drop by. There were even a few brothers down there from the other side of the tracks (how some of us referred to East Elmhurst). But Danny Baylor had taken his struggle to the Bronx High School of Science.

The high school *was* saving me. I didn't mind the three-hour daily commute, looked forward to the four or five hours of homework. The old crew didn't much get in the way. Corona never had a high school, so we were sent to various schools all over the borough. Flushing (where Sherry was), Bryant, Bowne, Long Island City, Woodrow Wilson (where Wallace was), Bayside, Newtown. Everyone had plenty new things to get into. Some were sent out of the state altogether. Down south, a remedy for urban waywardness a number of parents would attempt. They hoped the old could cure the new.

Most times when I walked up First Avenue to the school, that is, when I happened to come in by way of the Canarsie line, I would see this red-headed guy on the corner, one of the seniors, dressed in an army jacket and boots. He would be passing out or selling pamphlets or newspapers expounding the position of the left. There was always something about oppression and the military-industrial complex. Boone spoke about student radicals in the barbershop. He said they were all socialists while their parents were still footing the bills. Nonetheless, I was still surprised to find a guy like that down at Stuyvesant. I was hip to the Panther thing in the air, the fight for rights thing, the anti-war Ali thing. But students generally fretted most about their averages, SAT scores, what colleges they could gain entry to, what scholarships they could obtain. Although I never viewed our corner propagandist as a serious player, there was something about his presence that nagged me.

Before the term ended Martin Luther King Jr. was dead. I was sixteen, hadn't yet decided to participate in any actual protest demonstrations, and they already seemed quite beside the point.

I pulled my overall average up to within a fraction of 80 in just one year, topping off the performance with a perfect 100 on the Regents Examination in Geometry. My mother was pleased and proud, and I was clearly back in the race for college. I needed three more semesters of 90 plus grades to increase my overall average to at least 85; I had to nail those SATs early in my senior year. Then I would be in line for a shot at a noteworthy institution. Would make it too. If I could protect Raymond from Keith.

That summer I landed a job with the Neighborhood Youth Corps. I was sent out to Brooklyn to work in Livonia Yard helping to maintain subway cars. I received forty-five dollars per week, thirty-eight and change after taxes, which was all right back then. I could offer Moms a few dollars although she would never accept as long as she saw visible signs, like needed clothes, that I was using the money in positive ways.

Most of the other youth workers were from Brooklyn and other parts of Queens. This one guy, Melvin, was drawn to me immediately. He was friendly enough, but more competitive than friendly. Would have dominated if I didn't hold him at bay. After he bragged about how well he played basketball in tournaments out at Lincoln Park, I beat him easily one day during our lunch break. He said his jumpshot was off but he didn't exactly beg for a rematch. Then he used to say that Corona was nothing and I would invite him to come deliver that speech on Northern Boulevard.

Then he would want to box and I would tell him I didn't play with my hands, but if he wanted to get serious. . . . As initiation tests go, it was pretty easy and we were cool.

The only thing Melvin had on me streetwise was that he was using heroin. Snorting. That shouldn't have bothered me so much, but it did. I had done my share of abusing drugs by then while I was getting ready for high school — reefer, snaps, wine, cough syrup. But I hadn't done anything since I started Stuyvesant but smoke an occasional joint. The heroin plague had certainly reached the neighborhood, touching or about to touch my own circle of friends. However, I hadn't thought much about it until Melvin talked about getting high, never suggesting I try it, but hooking me all the while.

I vomited at first. Used a fingernail file to shovel a bag of the shit up my nose over at Gary's. Gary was weird, a bright guy who was somewhat new in the neighborhood. I couldn't understand why someone with only a year left at a highly regarded school like Brooklyn Tech would want to be fooling around with this stuff. He didn't understand me either.

When I went to work I couldn't wait to tell Melvin what I had done.

"So you put the thing in your nose, hunh?"

"That's what I just told you, ain't it?"

"Yeah well dig this. It's done but don't get crazy with it. Sit back, think about it. Think about what you doing, you know, dip and dab. You don't wanna catch no habit, no chippie."

I was snorting again that same night. And by that weekend, I was ready to hit the main line. Weird Gary, old standby Wallace, and I went down to 127 playground, which, although on the right side of the tracks, was becoming a major trade center for drugs.

"So get the money right" Gary said. "We want an organized move here. How many things we gettin in all?"

"I want two bags" I replied. "What they got down here, fours?"

"All depends on who we catch. They mostly got fours down here, but we might catch treys. I even heard there were some deuces around like uptown. But it's a rumor thing. We better just count on the fours."

I fished a ten from my pocket, the only money I had, and handed it to Gary. He got eight dollars from Wallace, who had his money partially wrapped around the soda can from which he was sipping, and gave me two of those.

"So we gettin six things" he uttered mostly to himself. "We straight."

After a few more strides Wallace broke in, "You sniffin these Keith? Or you gonna skin pop?"

"I don't know. I'm thinkin about poppin one and holding one. Supposed to feel it more, right?"

"Yeah, and feel it a lot quicker too."

"I may as well pop then. What you think, Gary? You Tech guys are supposed to be so smart though downtown we know you ain't nothin."

"Skin pop it man" he chuckled. "You can handle it."

So that's how we decided I'd take the next step down the snort-intramuscular injection-intravenous injection ladder. After Gary copped over by the handball courts, we cut across onto the baseball field and headed for the first base dugout. It was a spot secluded enough for our planned activity, yet with enough light coming from the nearby street lamp. As we approached the dugout we could see that someone had beaten us to the spot. Which actually didn't matter. They were neighborhood. We knew them. And there was room on the bench for all. In fact, I knew one of the guys too well. Another competitor, one with whom I shared a mutal dislike.

Everyone nodded ambiguous greetings and asked the muted rhetorical question: "What's happenin?" They were winding down their "operation get high" and we set about the task of firing up. Wallace went to rinse out the soda can at the water fountain. Gary pulled out his works. They were encased in aluminum foil and tucked inside an eyeglass case. I had seen them before. Glass dropper with the nipple from a baby's pacifier secured to the wide end with a rubber band. A small spike inside a plastic case. A bottle cap with a small wad of cotton inside and a bobby pin attached as a handle. Tough elastic string. Gary laid the works on the bench, gently unfolding the foil. He peeled the scotch tape off one of the glassine packets, unfolded the bag and dumped the dangerous dullish white powder into the bottle cap, the "cooker." He announced, "You're up first, Keith." This provoked the guy I disliked. He picked at me through Gary.

"What he doing? Maining? I know he ain't maining." Meaning I wasn't hip enough to shoot drugs intravenously like him. His speech was slurred. He slid a hand down inside his pants to scratch his groin, rubbing the side of his neck with the other hand. Gary ignored him but I reached over for the string and balled it up in my fist. By the time Wallace returned with the water, Gary had torn off a piece of the border on a dollar bill. He wet it in his mouth and wrapped it around the open end of the eyedropper. He jammed the spike, still in its cover, onto the dropper, shaking the instrument vigorously a few times to make sure the spike held. Then he drew about a half dropper of water from the can and squirted it into the cooker.

"This is Keith's shot" he announced in hushed tones to Wallace. "Gimme a light." Wallace already was pulling a book of matches from his pocket. He struck one and held the flame under the cooker. I had seen the procedure a couple of times by then, but I was fascinated anew by the chemistry involved. Wallace shielded the flame with one hand like a smoker trying to light a cigarette in the wind. Gary moved the cooker in a slow circular motion until he brought the contents to a simmer. He held the cooker with his left hand and had the homemade hypodermic in his right. He drew the mixture into the dropper by squeezing the nipple, inserting the tip of the needle into the cotton and releasing it, slanting the cooker a little so that all the fluid would run into the cotton.

I handed Wallace the string which prompted both him and Gary to stare at me in wonderment. The three of us knew you didn't need to tie up if you were only skin popping. Usually just took the injection back in the triceps area.

"What you doin?" Wallace asked.

"What it look like? Tie me up." I offered my left arm and after hesitating Wallace wrapped the cord around it a few inches above the elbow. As my arm wasn't very vascular, he had to loosen the tie and then retie it more firmly. Moving swiftly, Gary picked the vein running along the outside portion of the crook. He grabbed my arm, pressed his thumb hard against the chosen vein with a pulling downward motion, and deftly pricked the skin. Blood spurted up into the dropper. Wallace released the tourniquet and Gary squeezed the nipple to inject the shot. But he didn't sqeeze the nipple all the way, didn't want to shoot any air into the vein. He released the nipple and blood began flowing back into the dropper. This was called booting, was supposed to make you feel it quicker. I didn't need to boot much that night. The dropper was less than a quarter full when the shot hit me. A triple assault. Head spinning dizzily, mouth tasting the bitter quinine that was used as the cut, stomach hinting at turning over.

"Feel it?" Gary asked.

"Yeah" I whispered

Gary squirted the fluid back into the vein, this time squeezing the nipple all the way. As he removed the spike from my arm, he grabbed my arm just above the injection spot and pressed down on the vein so it hurt. He stroked the vein back in the direction of the injection spot, doing this to make sure to squeeze out any air bubbles. When he finished he headed over to the water fountain to rinse out the works. I sat dazed, head bowed, slightly rocking back and forth, stroking my vein in the manner that Gary had done, though not nearly as hard. The other group were collecting their belongings to slink away in agitated bops. I didn't catch the eye of the disliked one. And appearing, coming across the baseball field, was more neighborhood.

Melvin was a mainliner by the time the summer ended. And I had fallen deeper. On as slow a day as you could get in the streets, on one of those Sundays when wasn't no money happening for nobody, my nose started running and I got a few cramps in my stomach. As definite as registered mail, the chippie had arrived. I told myself what most novice addicts did: I could stop whenever I wanted. I didn't though. I took the whole conundrum back to the portrait of the peg-legged governor.

VII

Back at Stuyvesant I became obsessed with college. I daydreamed about it constantly, wishing I could forgo the final two years of high school. I even made certain practical moves.

Having a study period in my schedule, I volunteered to work in the college office under Mr. Wechsler whose son, in fact, was in my home-room section. I read all the information that came in about colleges, application procedures, standardized tests, scholarships, and other forms of financial aid. I wrote away for numerous catalogs to be sent to my home. At one time I thought my sister would benefit from them also since she was in her senior year, but she joined the maternity club and didn't make it out that term. I shared them with Gary who was rather disinterested. I think he knew he wasn't graduating either.

Heroin was the first thing that I feared could make me late. No, not like for a class, appointment, or job, but late in life. Although I hadn't always fulfilled my best capacities, I had still managed to make it on time to the places I needed to be. But you don't cheat dope for long. It collects its dues.

Gym classes were expressly participatory. We had to be in uniform every day and I didn't feel like being bothered with responding to Mr. Davis's ever-insistent urging to "move with alacrity." I dressed for gym sporadically, finally failing it. However, it was a minor subject and the grade wasn't computed as part of my academic average, so I really wasn't too upset. After all, I was holding on in the classroom. I could still keep much of my act going. Get down with Trigonometry and Chemistry and Hawthorne's *Scarlet Letter*. A 90 average was a thing of the past but I ran high eighties for the fall semester, which wasn't too shabby among the eager beaver, one-dimensional, no social concern types. They had no interest in the Mark Rudd parts of Columbia or the Free Speech Movement aspect of Berkeley.

Failing the gym class was just a warning of course. The overall inevitable decline soon followed. So that spring, while Ronald Reagan was sending the National Guard into Berkeley and imposing a curfew on the town, and Black students with guns held control of a building at Cornell, my main pursuit was for money for drugs.

I became involved in a series of crimes that initially ranged from purse snatching to burglary. Ripping off some White woman down in Jackson Heights, descending through the skylight of a cleaners or grocery store, squeezing through air ducts to plunder concession stands inside the airport, lifting television sets from those airport area motels where they hadn't yet been bolted down. It was convenient and sometimes crucial to have ready transportation, so stealing cars became part of the curriculum. You looked mostly for GM models. Back then GM was still using the old "turn ignition," the kind that could be activated without use of a key, that is, if the owner were careless. If he or she only turned the knob to the "off" position and not the "lock" position, you could start the car simply by turning the knob back to "on." At other times, you would take car keys obtained through various means and roam the streets trying them on like models. It never took long to find a fit. Sophistication wasn't necessary, no hot wiring or anything like that.

As the heroin plague infested the neighborhood, a network of petty gangsters was formed, daily circumstances of need and greed often determining which members of this network would get together on a given occasion. By being in the network you came to know who was reliable, who had heart, who was likely to snitch, who could stand the weight.

I was a pretty good wheel man by the summer of 1969. That July I had a shiny blue 1968 Oldsmobile Cutlass with a black vinyl top. One Saturday, in fact, the day before Man first walked on the moon, I handled a wheel job for a couple of local union members. Afterwards I got high, went to a couple of parties, and spread some favors around in case I needed to ask for some in the future. It was past four by the time I stashed the car and went home, only to find that I couldn't get in. Moms was enforcing her new regulation that if I didn't come home at a decent hour she would make sure I didn't get in. The rule was a good one. A seventeen-year-old had to have the wrong reasons for keeping the hours I wanted to keep, and some lessons had to be learned the hard way. That was an understanding and, I think, a strength my mother had. On the other hand, she hadn't grasped, and understandably so, the enormity of the problem with her son. First-generation northern urban youth were hard to figure.

I shrugged off my little housing problem and went back to fetch the Oldsmobile. Along the way I ran into Gary and a guy named Blue, so

the three of us went to the diner on Junction Boulevard and then over to
127. The sun had risen and I was wide awake. I had barely settled down
with the newspaper to read about the escapade to the moon when it started
to rain. I thought of running for the car, but instead I went along with
a suggestion to break into the school. We went through a front window
in full view of a man out walking his dog. As you might suspect, the
police arrived a few minutes later.

I was at a table in the cafeteria when I spotted the patrol car pulling
up along 25th Avenue. Calling to Gary and Blue, who were using their
newspapers as pillows, I dashed for the far exit. They scrambled for the
door near the window through which we had entered. Theirs was a poor
choice, I figured. Too close to the patrol car. However, the police apparently caught sight of me running toward the other exit and pulled the car
up to that door just as I was emerging. I spotted Gary and Blue getting
away. I ducked back inside and ran up a stairwell, finally settling into a
hiding place in the dark fourth floor gymnasium. It was to no avail. An
officer came in brandishing a flashlight and I was busted. He cuffed my
hands tightly behind my back, his partner said I smelled like a goat, and
they accused me of having stolen typewriters from the school for weeks.
I didn't say anything in response.

At the 114th precinct I was interviewed by a detective who seemed
primarily interested in my accomplices.

"O.K. pal, you want to tell me about the two guys who were with you?"

"What two guys?"

"Look buddy, I'm asking the questions. Understand?"

"I don't know them. I have seen them once or twice. But I don't know
their real names and I don't know where they live."

"O.K. It's your ass up the river by yourself." And that, surprisingly,
was it. No real pressure to make me squeal.

For arraignment I was taken over to Atlantic Avenue in Brooklyn.
Weekend court. I was placed in a cell by myself. As one of the legal aid
people was coming down the line to do the customary interviews, the man
in the next cell called me, though at first I didn't realize he was addressing
me in particular.

"Yo homes, next door. Next door, homes. You."

"You talkin to me?" I asked apologetically. But as soon as I asked the
question in that fashion I told myself to be more assertive, though not
defiant.

"Yeah man. You. You hear that punk comin down here for the info.
Fuck him. Don't tell him nothin. He ain't gonna do nothin for you. Askin
all them bullshit questions. What you got this time?"

This time? I wondered. I thought the veterans asked *"first time in kid?"* or something like that. Well, I sure wasn't going to give away that it was my first. What if my mother didn't show and I had to remain in this joint for awhile? It was a thought which just sneaked up and horrified me.

"Burglary" I responded, trying to make it sound like murder one.

"Yeah? Well don't tell this punk nothin cause he ain't doin nothin for you."

By this time the interviewer had reached this man's cell.

"I just want to ask you a few questions for the report."

"Man, get the fuck out of here. Who you kiddin? I got one bid in already. They droppin four armed robberies on me now. What kinda fuckin probation am I gettin? Or bail? Or any of that fuckin shit."

"But it's for your own good."

"Fuck you I said. Leave me the fuck alone." Then he called to me. "Don't tell em nothin youngblood."

"I have to" I told him, the words fluttering hesitantly from my mouth. "I can walk on this one. It's a meatball."

"Go ahead then" he advised after a pause. "But I'm tellin you homes, they ain't gon do nothin but fuck you up."

I was out early that afternoon. Paroled in the custody of my mother. Caught a legal aid attorney who happened to be a graduate of Stuyvesant High. He showed me his ring and said he couldn't understand what a fellow peg leg was doing in criminal court. So I sanitized the explanation as much as I could. Presented the whole matter as harmless mischief, that's all. Same way with Moms. Left the drug part out. Though in two more days she would know it all.

Wallace and I were on a fundraising mission. I still had the Cutlass and Wallace had a .22 revolver. I was no stickup kid but had confidence that we could handle something minor, you know, not get in over our heads.

Wallace had scouted a few sites down in Elmhurst and Woodside that he thought were worth another look. We picked up another local desperado named Tango, who was alleged to have enough nerve in matters like these, and were on the go, Wallace directing me to a Chinese laundry on 31st Avenue. We circled the block after passing the laundry, parking in the side block a car length or two shy of the avenue. There was a fire hydrant in front of us so the odds were we wouldn't get jammed in by another car. The getaway would be smooth. I left the keys in the ignition as Wallace and I exited the car. Then Tango got cold feet on us.

"I'll lay and get the seats ready."

"Seats ready?" Wallace exploded. "Man, what the fuck are you talking about? You suppose to be the lookout. Don't tell me you can see around corners."

"What's happening Wallace? I thought you double checked his references."

"Jay and them boys said he was cool. Fuck it. You still down?"

"Yeah." Wallace was already several yards ahead of me. I told Tango to wait right there.

There were no customers when we entered the laundry, only the woman behind the counter who had a fit when Wallace pointed the pistol at her. She began backing away slowly, shaking her head "no no no" with her hands pressed up against the sides of her face. She formed words with her mouth but no sound issued forth. I had leaned across the counter to open the cash register when a man came from the rear of the establishment. Upon seeing us his first impulse was to charge, but the image of Wallace leveling the pistol at him made him change his mind. He retreated, not with a look of fright, but as though he had an equalizer. I grabbed a small stack of bills and scooted out the door just ahead of Wallace. We sprinted around to the car, I fired up the engine, and we were in the bleachers at 127 in a matter of minutes. Tango was still with us but we ignored him until, after watching me divide the money evenly between Wallace and myself, he inquired, "What about me?"

"Should I shoot him?" Wallace asked me.

"Naw man," I replied, my mind on the real business at hand. "We ain't got time for that."

"Only take a second."

"Naw man, stop jiving." However, I wasn't totally convinced he was. Tango was quietly pathetic, what you might call a hope fiend.

The take was mostly singles, less than $20 altogether. We could get high but not complacent, and later that evening we were back on the prowl. This time we picked up Smitty, a bit undersized but generally game, although the pistol thing was new for him too.

We cruised out to Woodside to case a bakery, but it was too busy. We looked at a few drugstores and liquor stores but at least one of us would have an objection, would sense that something wasn't quite right. Frustrated, I began to think that my opinions were the only valid ones, that Wallace and Smitty were losing their heart.

Working back to the east, back through Corona-East Elmhurst, on through Flushing, we eventually wound up on Bell Boulevard in Bayside. There was a drugstore we all agreed was ripe for the picking. No one inside but the proprietor, chubby, balding, White, our type. Wallace and I approached the counter as Smitty stationed himself by the entrance.

"This is a stickup" my partner declared as I made my move for the register.

"Oh yeah?" the intended victim responded. Without flinching he reached down and drew a gun. Fortunately, my instincts had me backing away. The barrel of that gun seemed so huge he wouldn't have had to shoot to capture me. He could have lassoed me. By the time I turned to take full flight, Wallace and Smitty were scooting out of the door. If not for the situation I would have laughed at how they seemed to go through the doorway simultaneously, the doorway actually seeming to expand as in a cartoon.

We were entering Corona an hour or so later still not having made any money. As we rolled down Roosevelt Avenue up under the El train, we saw a White pedestrian entering the parking lot of Shea Stadium.

"Let's get him" Smitty suggested.

"Fine with me" I responded, slowing the car down only to speed up again when it turned out that the headlights of an approaching vehicle belonged to a patrol car. I held the Oldsmobile steady, tried to stay relaxed. I picked up the patrol car in the rearview mirror and watched it recede into the distance.

"Everything's cool" I reassured. "They ain't notice nothin." But the moment to hit the new target had been lost. I proceeded along Roosevelt. At the corner of 111th Street I spotted another White man descending the stairs leading from the train station.

"I'm getting him" I said impulsively and sprang from the car.

"No Keith no" I heard Wallace calling behind me. He was following me but I was gone. I pushed the man hard against the wall of a building.

"Now gimme that money!"

"Take it. Take it." he shrieked. As I went to empty his pockets a patrol car was screeching to the curb right behind us. This is what Wallace had been trying to warn me about. The instant I turned I could see the car almost hit Wallace who then started running back across Roosevelt. The man tried to grab me but I elbowed him viciously in the solar plexus, spinning around and following that up with a right cross to the jaw. He staggered, a cop was closing in, lights were swirling, I couldn't comprehend the shouting.

I took off down Roosevelt. As luck would have it, I happened to be on the longest block in the area. I could hear the cop behind me. That wasn't my major problem. Unless he were Bob Hayes in disguise, he didn't figure to be able to run me down. No, the major problem was that if the officer in the car chose to pursue me rather than Wallace, he could easily cut me off on the long straightaway.

Cutting into an alley, I encountered a high fence topped with a short row of barbed wire and didn't hesitate to scale it. I ripped my shirt going over but managed to jump down to the other side and scurry behind a clump of bushes just as the cop entered the alley.

"Freeze" he bellowed, his gun drawn. Hell, I wasn't planning to move at all. Figured I would blend into the scenery and make him think I had escaped. There was another fence to climb and no way I could make it.

He shined a flashlight. "Come out of those bushes with your hands up." I thought about trying to escape but with the losing streak I was on, I knew better than to count on a fence to block bullets. So I surrendered. The patrol car turned into the alley with no prisoner inside. Just me and the law again.

I was arraigned the next morning in Kew Gardens. The judge did a double take at my yellow sheet, realizing that my prior arrest had been only three days before.

"Appears as though he needs a rest" he considered before setting a cash bail of one thousand dollars.

My mother turned to me, repressed hurt and anger twisted together in her face, and whispered tersely, "I guess you're satisfied."

I used my phone privilege to call Uncle Howard, my best, perhaps only shot at bail. He said he would see what he could do. In the meantime I was on my way to Rikers Island, cell block 5, cell 5A6. Like most folks who made it to the Island, I turned reflective. I would lie on the top bunk staring at the red light bulb above the cell door mulling how I got to this part of the script, the trip, whatever. Got to the part with the stomach cramps. No sensationalized Hollywood gorilla jones stuff. Just a baby monkey thing I could handle. Every morning you could see at least one inmate with a strong habit, or maybe a weak constitution, fall out in the mess hall. Actually, you could have admitted to being a drug user on entering the facility, but that made you a registered addict in the new Rockefeller Program. There were early advantages for some in terms of medication and leniency, but the state kept more tabs and labels on you in the long run. Copping to the Rockefeller only made sense if you had a heavy beef, but if the beef were too heavy they wouldn't let you cop anyway.

Got to the part of worrying about time. After all, I was caught red-handed. Wasn't like I should waste the court's time and anger a district attorney by pleading innocent.

Got to the great reunion. Half the neighborhood was on the Rock. All the folks whose falls I had heard about and the ones whose disappearance I hadn't stopped running long enough to notice. Even old Lonnie Blair, who was all smiles when we ran into each other during a movement.

He broke from his line to greet me with a hug. The officer in charge let him get away with it.

Got to the around-the-clock fear. Avoiding direct eye contact but not shying away from it all the time either. Didn't want to issue challenges or have to accept any. But if I had to, I was committed to rumbling, to holding my own.

Conversations filled with lies echoing up and down the tiers. Ass kickings promised on the lockout. Landing in the day room watching news broadcasts monopolized by the trip to the moon.

I was supposed to be only fourteen months away from college. I had to get back on track. The dope game was a sucker play, not just in terms of lost opportunities. That was the obvious part. But more interesting was to understand drugs in terms of being controlled by others. This Black cop really made me see that one night on Northern Boulevard. He pounded his beat, taking his payola here and there, but he left a gem for me. He asked me had I ever seen any ocean liners dock in Flushing Bay or any 747s land on the Boulevard. Since I hadn't and told him so, he wondered how I didn't know that the only way I could get any heroin was because there were some people who wanted me to have it. It was not so much self-destruction that I was engaging in, but designed destruction.

By the time Uncle Howard came to get me I was ready to tell him, my parents, and anyone else who cared to listen what the hustle was all about and how I resolved to beat it. It's just that resolve didn't yet hold the upper hand with me.

VIII

I felt old for someone still in high school. Like if I did manage the course load, get a favorable disposition from the court, beat the latest phase of my drug involvement, and gain admission to college, I might be too worn out to attend.

A few of the brothers also started to age too much, began experimenting with heroin. I tried to discourage them as Melvin had done for me, but of course they didn't listen which, in one sense, was fine. They made my hustle safe and easy. You see, heroin usually cost more in their communities. So I would cop deuces in Corona, bring the supply to school, and give them a bargain. Give them two bags for seven, say, if they were used to fours. This would work until they traveled more and/or prices stabilized all over town. The few dollars generated were plentiful. I didn't have a habit. Knew I couldn't afford to ride that white pony hard with two cases already before the court. Besides, I really did talk to myself a lot about quitting.

Attempting to fit some productive activities in my schedule, I took a job uptown at the arcade next to the Apollo Theater. Needed to save for future educational expenses. At that point I didn't worry much about high school matters. I could do enough in class to get by and make sure my average didn't slip too far. No school official mentioned my legal problems so I assumed none of them knew how I had spent part of my summer vacation.

I scored a shade under 1200 on the SAT which wasn't too poor given the circumstances. And I sifted through my catalogs at home, focusing in on the University of Connecticut and the University of Notre Dame. My average was four or five points off what I desired, but because of my test scores and the fact that both schools were making highly publicized efforts to recruit Blacks, I managed to receive scholarship offers from both. Against the advice of my English teacher from the previous year, who thought the atmosphere would prove too constricting, I chose Notre Dame. Had visions of dusting off my athletic skills and becoming a scholar-athlete of renown.

During the fall semester I handled my academic subjects as expected. But I failed gym once again, my attendance being so spotty. This forced me into the position of taking back-to-back gym classes during the spring semester. On many occasions those were the only two classes for which I showed up. English was on my schedule after gym. When I bothered to stick around, I didn't really participate. I might ask why we couldn't discuss books like *The Outsider* and *Manchild in the Promised Land* only to get a retort about curriculum and classics. Sometimes I would sit at my desk in the back row (my usual position in all classes by then) and model social consciousness rhetoric into the form of the Shakespearean sonnet.

When I was off in my own world in class one day, a student in the next aisle patted my arm to get my attention and motioned toward the rear door of the classroom. I saw the big blond dean, Mr. McGinn, and my shop teacher, cool black-haired Mr. Valenti, peering through the thick glass. McGinn beckoned me and I responded while trying to figure out what he wanted. McGinn didn't frighten me. I had hookied too much, cut too many classes, had too much raw, real world experience to be shaken up by a high school dean. But although he couldn't scare me, he could antagonize me endlessly, warning me that I didn't have it made yet, that the school in Indiana was but a phone call away.

"Are you tired Raymond? It doesn't seem as if you're especially interested in English." His tone was matter-of-fact, not accusatory.

"Well you know" I replied while remaining civil. "I have those two gym classes."

"Are you sure that's it? Take a little stroll with us. It'll energize you."

"Energize?" I laughed. "I told you I am *enner-vated.*"

"Aw come on" Mr. Valenti intoned mildly. To myself I asked *what's the angle?* as I consented to walk.

When we came to an empty classroom, Mr. Valenti opened the door and McGinn asked me to step inside and take a seat. My mind was fully puzzled by then, but I didn't have to remain agitated for long. Clarity was cloaked in the dean's next request.

"Would you roll up your sleeves please?"

"What?"

"Would you roll up your sleeves?"

"For what? You think I'm a magician or something?"

However, the real question was how he finally put it together. *Observations? Probably where Valenti comes in. A court inquiry? A snitch?*

"Just roll them up" he snapped. Actually I didn't mind obeying his order. I wasn't carrying anything and was curious to see what they knew. However, in complying with McGinn's request I felt compelled to remind him that he didn't strike me as being the least bit intimidating.

"No problem" I stated while staring defiantly into his eyes.

I unfastened the cuff buttons on my shirt and rolled the sleeves up past the elbow. I thrust my arms forward in a gesture that indicated I had nothing to hide.

McGinn took my arm, the left one first, the one hardly ever pricked. Then he examined the right arm and saw, along the thickest vein, the pattern of needle marks, one as fresh as that morning, as well as the skin made dark and callous by prolonged puncturing.

"So you're using dope."

"Used to, which is not exactly the scoop of the year." Then I looked up at Mr. Valenti, who seemed mesmerized by my arm, and decided to lighten up. "As I said, I used to. But I stopped."

"What about these needle marks?"

"They're old" I said evenly. "Very old."

I'm sure McGinn didn't believe me, but he seemed confused. He took Mr. Valenti over near the door where they consulted in whispers, eventually deciding that I should be taken across the street to be examined at Beth Israel Hospital. Parental permission was required for this, so my father was called. I wasn't unnerved by all the fuss; I mean it wasn't like I was being arrested. I could go to Beth Israel Hospital as long as it didn't turn into Rikers Island while I was there.

I repeated my claims to the attending physician, which he received with professional detachment. He was primarily interested in whether I was presently under the influence, which I was not. He shined a light into my eyes, checked my reflexes, and had me sit in the emergency room for an hour or so before he informed me I was free to leave. That night I tried to ease my mother's worries. I told her I hadn't done any new wrong. Everything was old stuff.

The next day the guidance counselor, Mrs. Brody, called me in for a long talk. She was a nice person, engaging. This was serious talk. No sermonizing. Just a realistic look at things. She suggested I enroll as an outpatient at Greenwich House, a rehabilitation center over on 14th Street off Sixth Avenue. I walked over for the intake interview but didn't enroll.

I was around school less and less after that. Well on my way to a grand total of 56 official absences for the spring semester alone. Not to mention the classes cut after being marked present in homeroom. I didn't get interested in everyday attendance again until four students at Kent State University in Ohio were killed by the National Guard. There were demonstrations at the school and rallies over in Union Square. A relatively radical faction of students issued a demand for certain changes within the school and organized a student strike, which, in terms of numbers, was successful. In 1970 the spirit of the '60s had reached the White folks at Stuyvesant High. An assembly was called at which several instructors urged students to work through the system. Students blew off steam verbally. And in a few days it was back to business as usual although I don't recall that any concessions were made by the administration. Well, I already knew not to take White student activists too seriously. Boone had made me skeptical enough about that. But if I needed a more vivid reminder, the wait would not have been long. Five Black students were killed at Jackson State University in Mississippi, time for sho nuff demonstrations in my view, and the members of the relatively radical faction were too preoccupied with thoughts about graduation to interrupt classes again.

But not all the brothers were too busy. Several windows were smashed. The piano in the auditorium was set afire. Before stepping in line for their diplomas, they offered testimony as a new crop of eighteen year olds that Black martyrs also count.

After that particular fervor faded, I realized something that was perhaps the most incredible fact of my senior year. I still had a chance to graduate myself. I cleared court on the third of June, given youthful offender treatment, which meant that in return for my pleas of guilty my record would remain sealed if I encountered no further trouble with the law. My lawyer, proud of my scholarship, told me a joint or two was the best thing for loosening up. He said the hard stuff was strictly bad news.

The judge, after sentencing, instructed me to go to school, do well, and stay out of her courtroom. She sounded sincere.

I couldn't make any grades to speak of for the eighth semester, could sort of just squeak by the way I had left junior high school three years earlier. But classroom grades weren't the only concern at that point. Regents Examinations were required in several classes and there was a stipulation that students with more than 20 absences in a class would not be permitted to sit for an exam. However, Mrs. Brody pulled me over that hurdle, consulting all the parties involved in waiving the attendance requirement once I assured her I could pass the three exams I had to take.

I kept my end of the bargain. 82 in Physics. 79 in History. And English was the irony of ironies. There was an essay question on the overcrowded judicial system that I handled on the way to an 83. Despite passing the Regents, I was given a 40 in English, but it was decided at a special meeting that I would be given credit for the course and allowed to graduate. Time to bid old peg leg goodbye.

Advancing to college was another matter. I convinced myself that I would not show up on the campus of Notre Dame addicted to heroin. But the way I began to run the streets that summer, you would have thought I intended to kick on the bus ride to South Bend. I stole some more, did a little dealing, shot the highest dosages of dope I ever had. Jail was a more likely destination than a university.

Father Hepsburgh had his say on where I would be when he sent me a letter halfway through the summer canceling my admission. Said something about my not being ready for college at that time. No doubt he knew what he was talking about. But besides being angry, I wondered what the decision had been based on. Had my old adversary, the dean, tripped me with telephone wire? Did the folks out there know about the legal piece? Had it simply been the eighth semester grades or attendance?

My mother received the news stoically, probably thankful not to hear worse. I think my father had allowed himself to be more adventurous in his dreaming, so he appeared much more distraught. I tried to reassure him by telling him that although the past had caught up with me, I was in command of the present and would bounce back. Still make it. We called the University of Connecticut to see if the offer previously made could be reactivated. No chance. The scholarship had gone to someone else.

So there would be no college in September. After all those years putting in time with the White folks, they finally had the chance to leave me behind. That was bad enough, but I felt defeated among the brothers, especially in Corona, where I had been a bearer of collective hope. Sure we all ran together, but several of them depended on me not to be an authentic loser in the end. Like Wallace, for example, recent recipient of a three-year sentence for robbery. He kept writing to tell me to tighten up the school thing.

Fortunately, there was encouragement to be found in the streets also. I had a friend named Alan Jennings, tough survivor in his own right, who was on his way to Queensborough Community College. Whenever we would come across each other that summer, he would have a pep talk for me or some advice. He suggested I apply for February admission to Queensborough, put in a few good semesters, and reevaluate my academic position at that point. Naturally the drug use would have to cease and I twice tried to quit on my own. However, because I knew I had my biggest habit yet, as soon as I caught a cramp I became fearful and, fully cognizant of how weak I was, dove back into the cooker. It took a newspaper headline to yank me out for good.

On August 8th the paper blared in bold print the story of how Jonathan Jackson walked into a courtroom in California, announced that he was taking over and had come to free his brother, celebrated prison writer George Jackson, and got himself smoked during the subsequent shootout. Most people on the street were buzzing about the derring-do involved, the fireworks. Most poignant to me was that Jonathan was only seventeen years old. Here was a kid younger than I who put his very life on the line because he still believed in dreams. Had to believe in them, that is, if he really thought he could pull off such a stunt. I understood dreams, idealism. I understood living in the future. But the trick is to know when the future has arrived.

Almost as soon as I finished reading the story I knew I was out of the drug life. The truth of that proposition was as clear as the bright caps of angry ocean waves hurtling toward a shore in clear darkness. A rhythmically sparkling clarity to which one who is amid the turbulence of the sea would be blind. That afternoon I visited my father. After watching a baseball game on television I announced I was spending the night. Dad was at the post office by then working the night shift, and I was certain to have the solitude I needed when I invited that often feared jones to come on down.

Oh, the stomach cramps were there, the runny nose, the diarrhea, the chills alternating with outbursts of sweat. The first night was the worst of course, with no sleep to be had. But I rolled to and fro across the sheets, actually welcoming the struggle, the fluorescent peaks of those waves collapsing just before me. The images I hadn't gathered myself to decipher. Yo-yo heads bobbing up and down in nods of escapism decorating Northern Boulevard, Lenox Avenue, Eighth Avenue, Avenue D. Gorgeous women transformed into apparitions of slurred speech and desperate thighs. Everyone scratching, lazily slapping their own faces. Yellow-eyed hepatitis sufferers. The man who needed no needle because he kept holes in his arm large enough to drip dope into them directly from the dropper. Spike marks in necks. Alongside vaginas. On penises. Drops of blood on my diploma because I got careless while showing it off to win a bet. Shoving ice down Gary's drawers after an overdose. Shooting a salt shot in his arms, walking him back to consciousness.

I welcomed it all, the sight, the roar. Keith was going to college.

9
Conclusion

With a rap or two of the magistrate's gavel punctuating my junior high school experience, I reached new sociolinguistic heights. I had successfully wielded language as an instrument of power in the often-intimidating world of the legal system. This tactical success gave me greater confidence than ever in my ability to manage impression in novel situations, using language as the primary device, and it also served as dramatic notice of a truth I was well aware of by then: inadequate language skills would not be my downfall. By the close of eighth grade, with my reading level at a solid 12.2 according to my performance on the Metropolitan Achievement Exam and with a healthy 86 percentile ranking on the Iowa Test of Educational Development (see Table 4 in Appendix), I had moved far beyond any barrier constructed solely with Standard English. A major purpose of this book has been to describe this movement, yet this book is not simply about positive accomplishments. Contrary to what some might have anticipated, mastery of the standard dialect did not in and of itself lead to outstanding formal academic progress and, as the narrative indicates, I foundered badly.

My average in academic subjects dropped from 84 at the end of seventh grade to 79 at the close of eighth grade to 70 at the close of ninth grade. As indicated, I made a comeback upon entering Stuyvesant High, finishing the tenth grade with a 90.2 average for the spring semester. In the process of doing so I scored the previously reported 100 on the Regents Examination in Geometry, received a grade of 94 in English, and earned a 91 in Spanish II (after failing Spanish I with a 55 just one year earlier).

Then the heroin usage began and the grades plummeted once again. I averaged 78 for the latter half of my junior year and 61.7 the last half of my senior year, this last feat highlighted by the 40 in English and 56 general absences. I was torn between institutions, between value systems. At times the tug of school was greater, therefore the 90.2 average. On other occasions the streets were a more powerful lure, thus the heroin and the 40 in English and a brief visit to the Adolescent Remand Shelter (I couldn't talk my way out of that one.) I saw no middle ground or, more accurately, no total ground on which anomalies like me could gather. I tried to be a hip schoolboy, but it was impossible to achieve that persona. In the group I most loved, to be fully hip meant to repudiate a school system in which African-American consciousness was undervalued or ignored; in which, in spite of the many nightmares around us, I was urged to keep my mind on the Dream, to play the fortunate token, to keep my head straight down in my books and "make it." And I pumped more and more dope into my arms. It was a nearly fatal response, but an almost inevitable one.

Several recent and popular books can be used to shed further light on my predicament. In fact, *Hunger of Memory* by Richard Rodriguez (1983) helped motivate me to produce this present work. Rodriguez, a Mexican-American, reveals the storm of torment he has weathered in order to assimilate into the culture of mainstream America. He has chased the middle-class dream and caught it, but the psychic costs have been enormous, as he himself well knows. He has suffered alienation to the point of feeling apart from his own family, has virtually given up his native tongue, has zealously pursued the ideals of his upper-middle-class companions, has endured the caustic rebuttals of opponents who dislike his anti-affirmative action and anti-bilingual education views, and he has felt that all the pain has been worth it. Whether it has indeed been worth it is something only Rodriguez can decide, in fact, must decide, but he is mistaken to advocate an educational policy under which his type of pain is to be justified rather than prevented. Early on in his book he writes, "I remember what was so grievously lost to define what was necessarily gained" (p. 6); I immediately scribbled a question in the margin: But was it necessarily lost? The answer, however, is not easily arrived at. Of course it (his culture) was necessarily lost inasmuch as he chose to give it up. What one does is necessary in one's own eyes. But in a larger sense, we are asking if such cultural loss is a desirable aim of public education, and this question has only one answer: No! More specifically, getting back to the issue of language, the eradication of one tongue is not prerequisite to the learning of a second. Rodriguez participated in such self-annihilation *for as long as he did* because he thought it benefited him personally. It would be tragic, however, to translate his own appraisal of his pain into pedagogy.

Rodriguez asserts that: "Radical educationalists meanwhile complain that ghetto schools 'oppress' students by trying to mold them, stifling native characteristics. The truer critique would be just the reverse: not that schools change ghetto students too much, but while they may promote the occasional scholarship student, they change most students barely at all" (p. 68). If one has ever watched the gleam in the eyes of kindergarteners fade to smoldering anger before they even reach adolescence, if the children Kohl or Kozol or Levy or Fader or Collins has taught are at all real characters, then one knows all too much about some of the damaging changes that the public school system has wrought.

Rodriguez just ignores reality. His thinking is characterized by the failure to stretch his own arguments out to logical conclusions, by the passing off of his own transactional choices as outer-determined inevitabilities, again, by pushing his pain as policy instead of using it to question policy. One would expect him to fumble a disussion of Black English and, predictably, he delivers:

> I remember the black political activists who have argued in favor of using black English in schools. (Their argument varies only slightly from that made by foreign-language bilingualists.) I have heard "radical" linguists make the point that black English is a complex and intricate version of English. And I do not doubt it. But neither do I think that black English should be a language of public instruction. What makes black English inappropriate in classrooms is not something *in* the language. It is rather what lower-class speakers make of it. Just as Spanish would have been a dangerous language for me to have used at the start of my education, so black English would be a dangerous language to use in the schooling of teenagers for whom it reinforces feelings of public separateness. (pp. 33–34)

Rodriguez has surely hit upon a dilemma, one not to be taken lightly. But I think the most potentially dangerous thing concerning public education is to allow it to remain pretty much as it has been. Important works concerning language instruction, several of which I have cited thus far, contain quite clear warnings against suppressing students' language. Such action helps create failing students, provides an inadequate support system for scholarship students, and may promote within the latter group negative self-concepts. Rodriguez is aware of these dangers, particularly those involving scholarship students. After all, he was a victim himself. However, he doesn't see that part of the solution to the problem lies in using the children's own languages in school. He insists on cultural suicide, a conclusion totally unappealing to me, one I rejected as an adolescent.

John Edgar Wideman's book, *Brothers and Keepers* (1984), provides related insights. Wideman, whose career has been even more distinguished than that of Rodriguez, has lived through a similar process of cultural self-denial. Part of what makes his book more refreshing to me, though, is that he is still trying to come to grips with his personal history; he doesn't ask anyone to emulate him. Much of this critical self-examination is motivated by the guilt he feels over the fact that his brother is doing a life sentence for murder; nevertheless, his self-exploration is quite honest and revealing.

A question that keeps nagging Wideman is this: How could he and his brother, both from the same background, undergo such vastly different experiences? But actually the answer is not all that complicated. They had different visions. John, a child of the fifties, strongly identified with mainstream America and, like Rodriguez, he was willing to commit cultural suicide to gain membership. He writes:

> To get ahead, to make something of myself, college had seemed a logical, necessary step; my exile, my flight from home began with good grades, with good English, with setting myself apart long before I'd earned a scholarship and a train ticket over the mountains to Philadelphia. With that willed alienation behind me, between us, guilt was predictable. One measure of my success was the distance I'd put between us. Coming home was a kind of bragging, like the suntans people bring back from Hawaii in the middle of winter. It's sure fucked up around here, ain't it? But look at me, I got away. I got mine. I didn't want to be caught looking back. I needed home to reassure myself of how far I'd come. If I ever doubted how good I had it away at school in that world of books, exams, pretty, rich white girls, a roommate from Long Island who unpacked more pairs of brand-new jockey shorts and T-shirts than they had in Kaufmann's department store, if I ever had any hesitations or reconsiderations about the path I'd chosen, youall were back home in the ghetto to remind me how lucky I was. (p. 27)

I had no desire, as John did, to alienate myself from my community.

Robby Wideman, a child of the sixties, ten years John's junior, only fourteen months older than I, did not, as I did not, share his brother's aspirations. His adolescent perspective could be summed up as follows:

> In the real world, the world left for me, it was unacceptable to be "good," it was square to be smart in school, it was cool to be cold to your woman and the people that loved you. The things we liked we called "bad." "Man, that was a bad girl." The world of the angry black kid growing up in the sixties was a world in which to be in was to be out — out of touch with the square world and all of its rules on what's right and wrong. The thing was to make your own rules, do your own thing, but make sure it's contrary to what society says or is. (p. 58)

Robby's reasoning was the type of reasoning that often made sense to me. It was more than coincidence, therefore, that in the summer of 1968 we both took that hard fall down into the world of heroin addiction. Robby just didn't make it back in time to avoid prison.

No one paid more for the type of cultural conflict being discussed here than Edmund Perry. He lost his life. A teenager from Harlem, Perry finished four years at Phillips Exeter, one of the most prestigious prep schools in the country, only to be killed less than two weeks after graduation, allegedly during the act of mugging an undercover police officer. A cop's bullet canceled Edmund's full scholarship to Stanford University. Edmund's brother, Jonah, a student at Cornell University, was tried as an accomplice but was subsequently acquitted. During the furor surrounding the case, when the Perry boys were symbols of general Black rage directed at the police department or useful icons for self-serving types, one thing became increasingly clear. Not many people, especially Blacks, allowed for the complexity of Edmund or Jonah. Reporter Robert Sam Anson (1987) illustrates this point well in *Best Intentions*. The argument that scholarship students couldn't be involved in street crime is a shallow conception. I happen to think the Perrys were guilty. I was saddened by the event but not surprised at all. The very day Edmund Perry died I took my oral examinations at New York University. As the last step in earning a doctorate in English Education, I was called upon to discuss much of the information contained in the book now before you.

It is significant to note that many of the students Anson interviewed at Exeter said that Edmund was too hung up on "Blackness," said that they had grown tired of hearing it. Easy enough for them to say, it wasn't their immediate problem. Many educators, however, must continue to listen. Edmund Perry wasn't the last person to suffer a kind of enforced educational schizophrenia, and the world is a more complex place than a Michael Jackson video in which the Harlem-boy-at-prep-school dilemma is resolved with a series of sublime dance steps capped by a sermon. As part of the present movement for educational reform, along with the call for increased salaries, professionalization, greater teacher input in shaping curriculum, mandatory preschool, less powerful bureaucracies, and so on, there must be an insistence that educators understand and indicate by their actions the importance of cultural and linguistic pluralism in educational settings. Why fight for better salaries for teachers so they can do a higher paid job of alienating and attempting to eradicate?

That teachers break the confines of monoculturalism is more crucial than ever before. It has been suggested in some circles, given the history of Black-White classroom confrontations, that the solution is an increase in the number of African-American teachers. If such candidates were not into cultural self-denial (a phenomenon too widespread), it seems a reasonable remedy and, indeed, there is no question that the recruitment of minority teachers should be a priority. Nonetheless, current data show that the percentage of African-American public school teachers is decreasing and probably will continue to do so. Whitaker (1989) reports that because of low pay, undesirable work conditions, and overall frustration with school systems, African-Americans are shunning careers in education. It is predicted, he reveals, that by the turn of the century 40 percent of the students in public schools will be Black while less than 5 percent of the teachers will be so.

Aside from this specific concern, demographics indicate that schools all over the nation are becoming more and more ethnically diverse. Raspberry (1988) reports that ethnic diversity is potentially upsetting to the "civic paradise" of Minneapolis-St. Paul: "For the first time, whites are on the way to becoming a minority in Twin Cities public schools. The new immigrants include Filipinos, Vietnamese, Hmong from Laos and an influx of blacks quite different from the upwardly mobile managers, technicians and educators the area is used to dealing with" (p. 3B).

As this whole educational enterprise proceeds inexorably but unsteadily toward the twenty-first century, language educators in particular must prepare themselves to function productively in multicultural classrooms. Terry Dean (1989) has suggested specific techniques that may be useful. Having worked with students from over thirty ethnic groups, he assigns writing topics about culture itself, about language itself, to ensure that student-centered discussions of difference, collision, and assimilation, are central to the course of study. Dean understands that "how students handle the cultural transitions that occur in the acquisition of academic discourse affects how successfully they acquire that discourse" (p. 23). Add a multicultural literature to the mix and you have a good start toward a model language arts classroom.

Over the years, roughly 85 percent of Dean's students have expressed the belief that they do not have to give up their home and cultural values to succeed in school. This has been the attitude of thousands of African-Americans all along. What has been commonly referred to by educators as "failure" to learn Standard English is more accurately termed an act of resistance: Black students affirming, through Black English, their sense of self in the face of a school system and society that deny the same. It is not at all shocking to me, as it was to many, that a more recent study by Labov (see Stevens 1985) demonstrates that the language of many Blacks is diverging more and more from Standard English. With continued lack of equal opportunity in many areas, with increased racial polarization, only those who underestimate the significance of language as a symbol of protest or group solidarity could expect otherwise.

It can be said that the cultural conflict that has confronted African-Americans in schools "got me later," as it did Robby Wideman and Edmund Perry. However, it finished off many students "sooner," caused them to shrink away from formal education before they could gain or, more importantly, even appreciate the enormous power to be had through encounters with a wide variety of books, of articles, of conversations, and, by way of writing, through encounters with their innermost selves. These students were helped to fail before they could fully develop the sociolinguistic ability necessary to educate themselves.

. . . and mostly they lead marginal lives of regret and self-blame and eventually they preach to their children about, uh hunh, the virtues of the school system. . . .

I have tried to show in this book that language instruction and school education in general can only be a widespread success, in the humanitarian sense of the word, when teachers stop assuming that students are inferior and/or have nothing to contribute to the educative process other than to sit and absorb. I don't know all that must be done, however, to break the cycle of failure. But to successfully challenge current practices that justify eradicationist attempts aimed against African-American identity and the language variety in which that identity is most clearly realized is a worthwhile place to begin.

Appendix: Records

Tables 1–4 have been retyped because the print quality of the original documents is too poor for reproduction purposes.

TABLE 1   Guidance Data

Date	Outstanding Abilities
6–64	Raymond is an eloquent speaker and very much interested in social studies. He is also a fine athlete.

Date	Outstanding Disabilities
6–61	Father not living with family. Raymond needs supervision.

Date	Outstanding Interests
6–63	Poetry – Creative writing.

TABLE 2

PERSONALITY		CLASS								
(Check one in each group with an X)		K-1	1-1	1-4	1-3	2-1	3-1	4-1	5-1	6-1
RELATIONSHIP TO OTHER CHILDREN	A. Works and plays well with others.	X	X	X	X			X	X	X
	B. Does not get along well with others.					X	X			
ATTITUDE TOWARD GROUP CONTROL	A. Usually non-conforming.									
	B. Occasionally resents group control.	X				X	X	X	X	X
	C. Responds well to group control.		X	X	X					
LEADERSHIP	A. Good leader, accepted by others.	X	X						X	X
	B. Fair leader on occasion.			X	X	X	X	X		
	C. Does not possess leadership qualities.									
RESPONSIBILITY	A. Usually not dependable.									
	B. Occasionally evades responsibility.					X	X	X	X	X
	C. Usually dependable.	X	X	X	X					
NEED FOR ATTENTION	A. Requires inordinate amount of attention.									
	B. Satisfied with reasonable amount of attention.	X	X	X	X	X	X	X	X	X
STABILITY	A. Usually well controlled.	X	X	X	X	X	X	X	X	X
	B. Occasional temper outbursts.									
	C. Frequent temper outbursts.									
AGGRESSIVENESS	A. Does not assert himself.									
	B. Moderately aggressive.	X	X	X	X	X	X	X	X	X
	C. Over-aggressive, fights frequently.									
SOCIAL PARTICIPATION	A. Shy, withdrawn, does not participate.									
	B. Participates actively in group projects.	X	X	X	X	X	X	X	X	X
SELF CONFIDENCE	A. Usually works with confidence.	X	X	X	X	X	X	X	X	X
	B. Needs frequent encouragement.									
	C. Lacks confidence, needs constant encouragement.									
ACTIVITY	A. Usually lethargic.									
	B. Normally energetic.	X	X	X	X	X	X	X	X	X
	C. Usually restless, hyperactive.									
WORK HABITS	A. Rarely attends to work.									
	B. Generally works with sustained attention.									
	C. Works with sustained attention.	X	X	X	X	X	X	X	X	X
INITIATIVE	A. Frequently makes original contribution.	X	X	X	X	X	X	X	X	X
	B. Requires direction.									
NERVOUS HABITS	A. Has numerous nervous habits.									
	B. Is relatively free of nervous habits.	X	X	X	X	X	X	X	X	X
RELATIONSHIP TO PARENTS	A. Seems free in relationship to parents.	X	X	X	X					
	B. Parent-child relationship seems disturbed.					X	X	X	?	

TABLE 3

	YEAR BEGINNING	SEPT 1957	SEPT 1958	SEPT 1959	SEPT 1959	SEPT 1959	SEPT 1960	SEPT 1961	SEPT 1962	SEPT 1963
LANGUAGE ARTS	READING		S	S	S	S	S	E	E	E
	WRITTEN COMMUNICATION					S	S	G	E	E
	SPELLING					S	S	G	E	E
	HANDWRITING			S	S	S	S	G	E	E
	ORAL COMMUNICATION	S	S	S	S	S	S	G	G	E
	APPRECIATION (LITERATURE GRADE 7 & 8)					S				
	GENERAL RATING					S	S	G	E	E
SOCIAL LIVING			S	S	S	N	N	F	F	G

S = Satisfactory G = Good E = Excellent F = Fair N = Needs Improvement

TABLE 4 Examinations

Date	Exam	Result
10-65	Iowa	86th percentile composite score
1-65	Met. Rdg.	11.0
10-65	Met. Rdg.	12.4
5-66	Met. Rdg.	12.2
4-67	Met. Rdg.	12.3

FIGURE 1

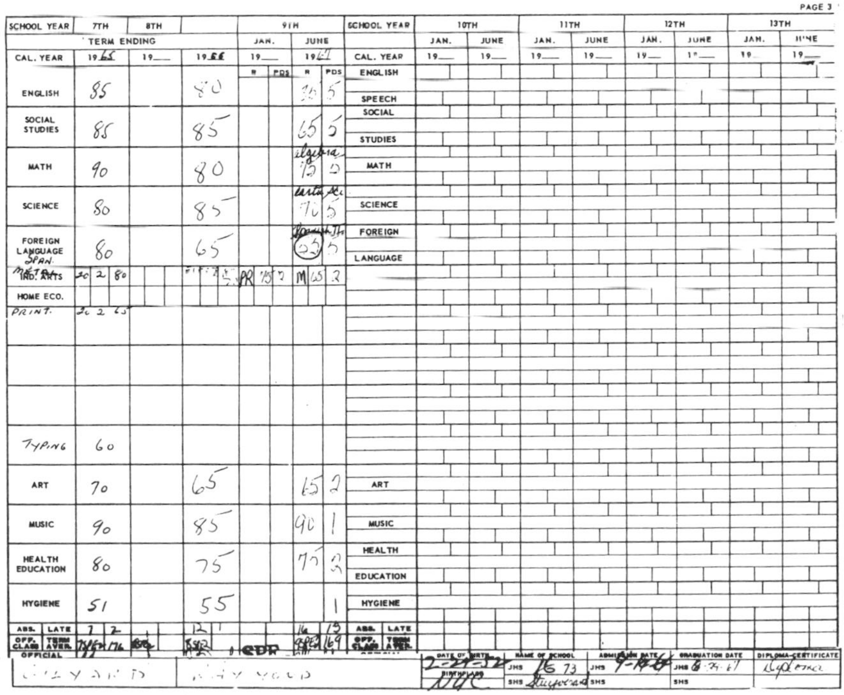

PAGE 3

SCHOOL YEAR	7TH	8TH		9TH JAN.	9TH JUNE
CAL. YEAR	1965	19__	1966	19__	1967
ENGLISH	85		80		70 5
SOCIAL STUDIES	85		85		65 5
MATH	90		80		algebra 75 5
SCIENCE	80		85		earth sci. 70 5
FOREIGN LANGUAGE SPAN.	80		65		55 5
METAL IND. ARTS	20 2 80			PR 75 2	M 65 2
HOME ECO.					
PRINT.	20 2 65				
TYPING	60				
ART	70		65		65 2
MUSIC	90		85		90 1
HEALTH EDUCATION	80		75		75 2
HYGIENE	51		55		1
ABS. LATE	7 2		12 1		16 13
OFF. CLASS TERM AVER.					169

DATE OF BIRTH 2-21-52 BIRTHPLACE NYC · NAME OF SCHOOL JHS 73 SHS Stuyvesant · ADMISSION DATE JHS 9-?-64 · GRADUATION DATE JHS 6-?-67 · DIPLOMA-CERTIFICATE diploma

FIGURE 2

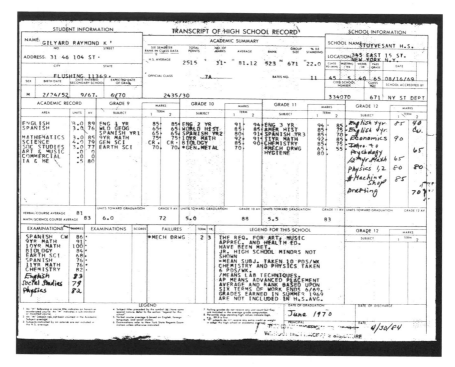

References

Anson, R. S. 1987. *Best intentions: The education and killing of Edmund Perry*. New York: Random House.

Baratz, J. C. 1969. Who should do what to whom . . . and why? *Florida FL Reporter* 7 (Spring/Summer): 75–77, 158–59.

Beck, M. S. 1979. *Baby talk: How your child learns to speak*. New York: Plume.

Bereiter, C., & Engelmann, S. 1966. *Teaching disadvantaged children in the preschool*. Englewood Cliffs, NJ: Prentice-Hall.

Bissex, G. L. 1980. *Gnys at wrk: A child learns to write and read*. Cambridge, MA: Harvard Univ. Press.

Britton, J. 1972. *Language and learning*. Harmondsworth: Penguin. Originally published 1970.

Britton, J. 1982. English teaching: Retrospect and prospect. In *Prospect and retrospect: Selected essays of James Britton*, ed. G. M. Pradl, 201–15. Montclair, NJ: Boynton/Cook. Reprinted from *English in the eighties*, papers presented at the Third International Conference on the Teaching of English, Sydney, 1980.

Burling, R. 1973. *English in black and white*. New York: Holt, Rinehart and Winston.

Byers, P., & Byers, H. 1972. Nonverbal communication and the education of children. In Cazden et al., 3–31.

Cazden, C. B., V.P. John, & D. Hymes, eds. 1972. *Functions of language in the classroom*. New York: Teachers College Press.

Chomsky, N. 1957. *Syntactic Structures*. The Hague: Mouton.

Chomsky, N. 1972. *Language and mind*. Rev. ed.. New York: Harcourt, Brace and Jovanovich.

Collins, M., & Tamarkin, C. 1982. *Marva Collins' way*. Los Angeles: Tarcher.

Corbett, E. P. J., ed. 1974. Students' right to their own language. *College Composition and Communication* 25 (Fall). Special issue.

Dean, T. 1989. Multicultural classrooms, monocultural teachers. *College Composition and Communication* 40 (1): 23–37.

Dillard, J. L. 1973. *Black English: Its history and usage in the United States*. New York: Vintage. Originally published 1972.

Eisner, E. 1981. On the differences between scientific and artistic approaches to qualitative research. *Educational Researcher* (April): 5–9.

Elgin, S. H. 1979. *What is linguistics?* 2d ed. Englewood Cliffs, NJ: Prentice-Hall.

Fader, D. 1971. *The naked children.* New York: Macmillan.

Fishman, J. A., & Leuders-Salmon, E. 1972. What has the sociology of language to say to the teacher? On teaching the standard variety to speakers of dialectal or sociolectal varieties. In Cazden et al., 67–83.

Flesch, R. 1955. *Why Johnny can't read — And what you can do about it.* New York: Harper & Row.

Flesch, R. 1983. *Why Johnny still can't read: A new look at the scandal of our schools.* New York: Harper Colophon.

Geertz, C. 1973. *The interpretation of cultures.* New York: Basic Books.

Goffman, E. 1959. *The presentation of self in everyday life.* Garden City, NY: Doubleday Anchor.

Goodman, K. S. 1967. Reading: A psycholinguistic guessing game. *Journal of the Reading Specialist* 4: 126–35.

Greer, C. 1976. *The great school legend: A revisionist interpretation of American public education.* New York: Penguin. Originally published 1972.

Haskins, J., & Butts, H. F. 1973. *The psychology of Black language.* New York: Barnes & Noble.

Holdaway, D. 1979. *The foundations of literacy.* Sydney: Ashton Scholastic.

Hudson, R. A. 1980. *Sociolinguistics.* Cambridge: Cambridge Univ. Press.

Isakson, R. L. 1979. Cognitive processing in sentence comprehension. *Journal of Educational Research* 72: 160–65.

Jensen, A. R. 1969. How much can we boost IQ and scholastic achievement? *Harvard Educational Review* 39: 1–123..

Joiner, C. W. 1979. Memorandum opinion and order on civil action 7-71861, Martin Luther King Junior Elementary School children et al. vs. Ann Arbor School District Board. 473 F. Supp. 1371 (E. D. Mich. 1979).

Jones, R. 1982. What's wrong with Black English. *Newsweek,* December 27, p. 7.

Kelly, G. A. 1963. *A theory of personality: The psychology of personal constructs.* New York: Norton.

Kohl, H. 1968. *36 children.* New York: Signet. Originally published 1967.

Kozol, J. 1968. *Death at an early age.* New York: Bantam.

Labov, W. 1972. *Language in the inner city: Studies in the Black English Vernacular.* Philadelphia: Univ. of Pennsylvania Press.

Labov, W. 1981. *The study of nonstandard English.* Rev. ed. Urbana: NCTE.

Levy, G. E. 1970. *Ghetto school: Class warfare in an elementary school.* Indianapolis: Pegasus.

Martin, N., Williams, P., Wilding, J., Hemming, S., & Medway, P. 1976. *Understanding children talking.* Harmondsworth: Penguin.

Mayher, J. S., Lester, N., & Pradl, G. M. 1983. *Learning to write/writing to learn.* Upper Montclair, NJ: Boynton/Cook.

McCracken, G., & Walcutt, C. C. 1963. *Basic reading: Teacher's edition for the pre-primer and primer.* Philadelphia: Lippincott.

O'Neil, W. 1973. The politics of bidialectalism. In *Black language reader* ed. R. H. Bentley & S. D. Crawford, 184–91. Glenview, IL: Scott, Foresman. Reprinted from *The Politics of Literature*, ed. L. Kampf & P. Lauter, Random House, 1970.

Penalosa, F. 1981. *Introduction to the sociology of language*. Rowley, MA: Newbury.

Perkins, E. 1975. *Home is a dirty street: The social oppression of Black children*. Chicago: Third World Press.

Perkinson, H. J. 1977. *The imperfect panacea: American faith in education. 1865–1976*. 2d ed. New York: Random House.

Philips, S. U. 1972. Participant structures and communicative competence: Warm springs children in community and classroom. In Cazden et al., 370–94.

Purkey, W. W. 1970. *Self concept and school achievement*. Englewood Cliffs, NJ: Prentice-Hall.

Raspberry, W. 1988. 'Diversity' changing twin cities' schools. *St. Louis Post-Dispatch*, November 21, 3B

Rodriguez, R. 1983. *Hunger of memory: The education of Richard Rodriguez*. New York: Bantam. Originally published 1982.

Rogers, C. 1982. *A social psychology of schooling*. London: Routledge & Kegan Paul.

Rosenthal, R., & Jacobson, L. 1968. *Pygmalion in the classroom*. New York: Holt, Rinehart and Winston.

Rouse, J. 1978. *The completed gesture: Myth, character and education*. NJ: Skyline Books.

Sledd, J. 1973. Doublespeak: Dialectology in the service of Big Brother. In *Black language reader*, ed. R. H. Bentley & S. D. Crawford, 191–214). Glenview, IL: Scott, Foresman. Reprinted from *College English*, January 1972.

Sledd, J. 1983. In defense of students' right. *College English* 45: 667–75.

Smith, F. 1971. *Understanding reading*. New York: Holt, Rinehart and Winston.

Smith, F. 1979. *Reading without nonsense*. New York: Teachers College Press.

Smith, F. 1980. Making sense of reading—And of reading instruction. In *Thought & language/language and reading*, ed. M. Wolf, M. McQuillan, & E. Radwin, 415–24). Cambridge, MA: Harvard Educational Review. Reprinted from *Harvard Educational Review*, 1977.

Smitherman, G. 1977. *Talkin and testifyin: The language of Black America*. Boston: Houghton Mifflin.

Spache, G. 1964. *Reading in the elementary school*. Boston: Allyn and Bacon.

Stevens, W. K. 1985. Study finds Blacks' English increasingly different. *New York Times*, March 15, A14.

Stewart, W. A. 1969. Urban negro speech: Sociolinguistic factors affecting English teaching. *Florida FL Reporter* 7 (Spring/Summer): 50–53, 166. Reprinted from *Social Dialects and Language Learning*, 1965.

Taylor, D. 1983. *Family literacy*. Exeter, NH: Heineman.

Troike, R. C. 1972. Receptive bidialectalism: Implications for second-dialect teaching. In *Language and cultural diversity in American education*, ed. R. D. Abrahams & R. C. Troike, 305–10. Englewood Cliffs, NJ: Prentice-Hall.

Trudgill, P. 1974. *Sociolinguistics: An introduction*. Harmondsworth: Penguin.

Whitaker, C. 1989. The disappearing black teacher. *Ebony*, January, 122–26.

Wideman, J. E. 1984. *Brothers and keepers*. New York: Holt, Rinehart and Winston.

Williams, F. 1973. Some research notes on dialect attitudes and stereotypes. In *Language attitudes: Current trends and prospects,* ed. R. W. Shuy & W. Fasold, 113–28). Washington, DC: Georgetown Univ. Press.

Wright, R. 1966. *Black boy: A record of childhood and youth.* New York: Harper & Row. Originally published 1945.

Index